A gift for:

From:

Other books in this series:
Wisdom 365 · Giggles 365 Days · Friendship 365 · Calm Days
365 Happy Days · For My Sister 365 · Chinese Wisdom 365 · Mother 365 Given with love

Published in 2018 by Helen Exley Giftbooks in Great Britain.
Illustrated by Juliette Clarke © Helen Exley Creative Ltd 2011.
Selection and arrangement by Dalton Exley © Helen Exley Creative Ltd 2011.
Dedicated, with all my love, to Lisa Fajembola.

ISBN: 978-1-78485-177-4

12 11 10 9 8 7 6 5 4 3 2

Acknowledgements: The publishers are grateful for permission to reproduce copyright materials. Whilst every effort has been made to trace copyright holders, we would be pleased to hear from any not here acknowledged.
DIANA ACKERMAN: From A NATURAL HISTORY OF LOVE by Diane Ackerman, copyright © 1994 by Diane Ackerman. Used by permission of Random House, Inc. BASIA: from the song 'Reward' by Basia. STEVE BOWKETT: with kind permission from Steve, who has dedicated his words to his lovely wife, Wendy. Find out more about Steve at www.stevebowkett.co.uk. SARAH BAN BREATHNACH: from Simple Abundance, with kind permission from Sarah Ban Breathnach.ORIAH MOUNTAIN DREAMER: by Oriah from THE INVITATION © 1999. Published by HarperONE, San Francisco. All rights reserved. Printed with permission of the author. www.oriah.org. CHARLES GHIGNA: from LOVE POEMS by Charles Ghigna © 2011. TONY HAWKS: comedian and author – www.tony-hawks.com, www.roundirelandwithafridge.com. MONKS OF NEW SKETE: with kind permission from The Monks of New Skete. JOANNA CAMPBELL SLAN: author – www.JoannaSlan.com. SOBONFU SOMÉ: copyright © 1997 by SOBONFU SOMÉ. Reprinted by permission of HarperCollins Publishers. NICHOLAS SPARKS: from The Rescue, with kind permission from Grand Central Publishing. MARIANNE WILLIAMSON: from A RETURN TO LOVE, www.marianne.com.

Helen Exley Giftbooks, 16 Chalk Hill, Watford, Herts WD19 4BG, UK.
www.helenexleygiftbooks.com

January 1

Loving someone and having them love you back is the most precious thing in the world.

NICHOLAS SPARKS, FROM "THE RESCUE"

WHAT IS A HELEN EXLEY GIFTBOOK?

Helen Exley Giftbooks cover the most powerful relationships: the love between couples, and the bonds within families or between friends. A very strong theme in Helen's recent books has been that of friendship and enduring relationships. Her team of researchers spare no expense in making sure each book is as thoughtful and meaningful as it is possible to create; good to give and good to receive. You have the result in your hands. If you find the quotes in *Love 365* helpful, please tell others. There is no power like word-of-mouth recommendation.

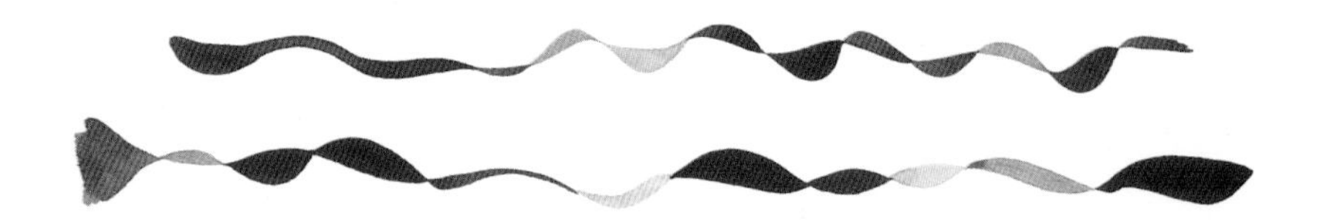

January 2

Time and love,
those are
the greatest gifts
of all.

TONY HAWKS

December 31

'Tis love, 'tis love, that makes the world go round!

LEWIS CARROLL (1832-1898),
FROM "ALICE'S ADVENTURES IN WONDERLAND"

January 3

That is true love which always and forever remains the same, whether one grants it everything or denies it everything.

JOHANN WOLFGANG VON GOETHE
(1749-1832)

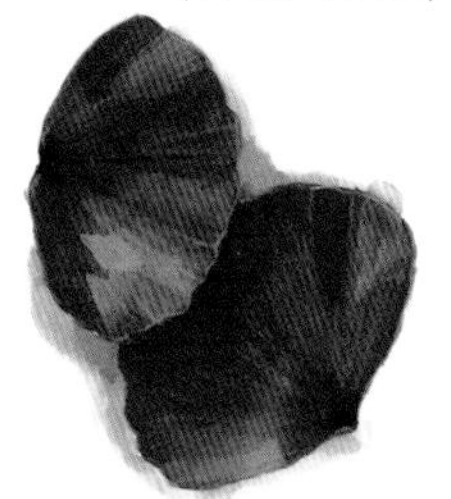

December 30

The only thing we'll be remembered for when we die is the love we leave behind.

ELISABETH KÜBLER-ROSS (1926-2004)

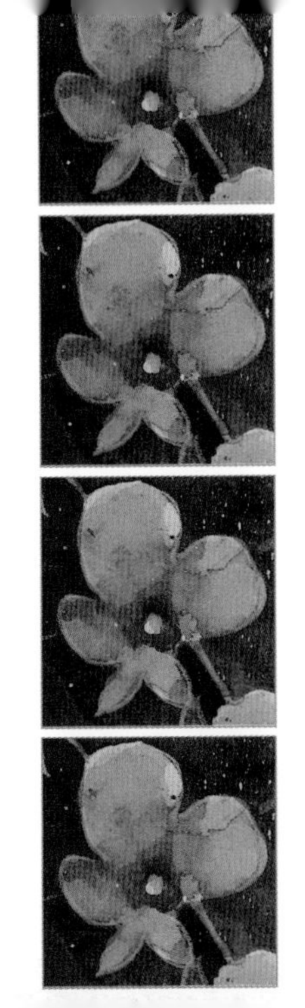

January 4

Eventually
you will come to understand
that love heals everything,
and love is all there is.

GARY ZUKAV

December 29

I can face anything with my hand in yours.

PAM BROWN, B.1928

January 5

Love is the greatest thing in the world.

OSCAR WILDE (1854-1900)

December 28

Love changes everything.

LINDA MACFARLANE, B.1953

January 6

Only here, only in each
other's arms,
we rediscover joy.
Only here we are ourselves,
and so each other's.

PAM BROWN, B.1928

December 27

I love thee to the depth
and breadth and height
My soul can reach....
I love thee with the breath,
Smiles, tears, of all my life!

ELIZABETH BARRETT BROWNING
(1806-1861)

January 7

I want you for always – days, years, eternities.

ROBERT SCHUMANN (1810-1856), TO CLARA WIECK

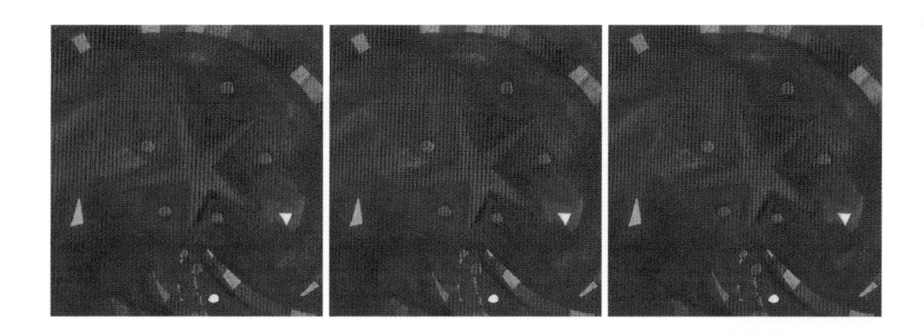

December 26

All my soul follows you,
love – encircles you –
and I live in being yours.

ROBERT BROWNING (1812-1889)

January 8

No one knows our secret.
We seem such an ordinary couple.
How could they know the depth
and wonder of our love?

BRIAN E. WILLIAMS, B.1961

December 25

Never lose a chance to tell someone you love them!

FROM "THE FRIENDSHIP BOOK OF FRANCIS GAY"

January 9

THE KEY TO LOVE
IS FAITH –
AND BEING ABLE TO TRUST
THOSE WHOM WE LOVE
AND WHO LOVE US.

STUART REININGER

December 24

Who would not welcome
anyone whose heart
is filled with nothing but love?

VINOBA BHAVE (1895-1982)

January 10

All I have is your love.
I have everything.

STUART & LINDA MACFARLANE

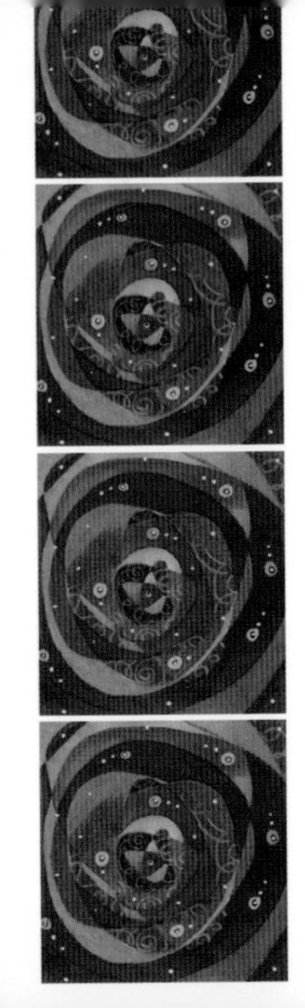

December 23

Immature love says:
"I love you because I need you."
Mature love says:
"I need you because I love you."

ERICH FROMM (1900-1980)

January 11

Love is not consolation, it is light.

SIMONE WEIL (1909-1943)

December 22

I never see beauty without thinking of you or scent happiness without thinking of you. You have fulfilled all my ambition, realized all my hopes, made all my dreams come true.

SIR ALFRED DUFF COOPER (1890-1954),
TO HIS FUTURE WIFE DIANA

January 12

Fair is the white star of twilight,
and the sky cleaner
At the day's end;
But she is fairer, and she is dearer,
She, my heart's friend!

SHOSHONE LOVE SONG

December 21

Love is something
that you can leave behind
when you die.
It's that powerful.

JOLIK (FIRE) LAME DEER ROSEBUD (LAKOTA)

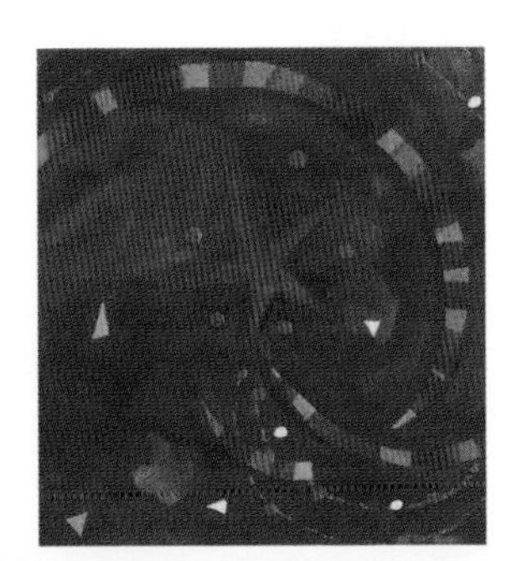

January 13

All, everything that I understand, I understand only because I love.

LEO TOLSTOY (1828-1910)

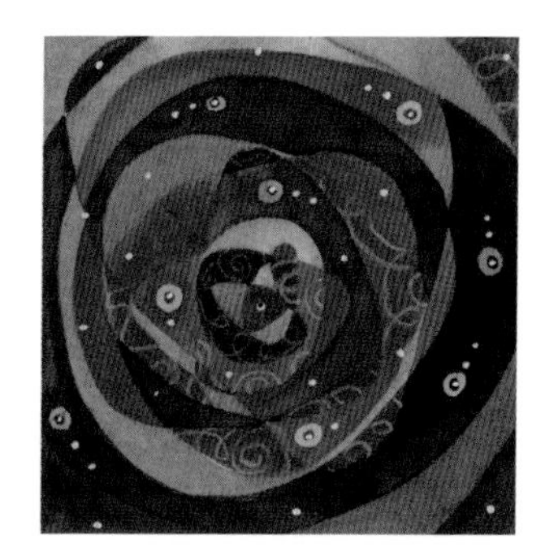

December 20

We live by admiration, hope and love...especially love.

FROM "THE FRIENDSHIP BOOK OF FRANCIS GAY"

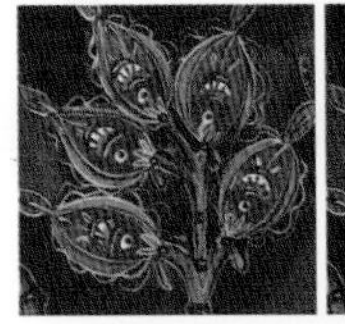    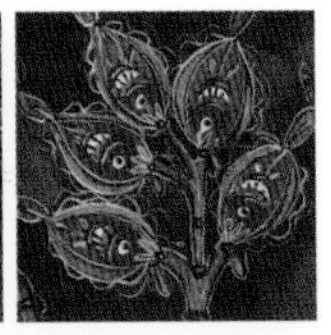

January 14

If the soul is to know itself
it must look into a soul.

GEORGE SEFERIS,
FROM "MYTHISTOREMA: POEM IV"

December 19

They are closest to us
who best understand what life
means to us, who feel for us
as we feel for ourselves,
who are bound to us in
triumph and disaster, who break
the spell of our loneliness.

HENRY ALONZO MYERS

January 15

WHEN IT COMES DOWN TO IT,
WE ALL JUST WANT TO BE LOVED.

JAMIE YELLIN

December 18

To love is to forgive,
to understand,
to wish the other's happiness....

ANAÏS NIN (1903-1977)

January 16

Beauty is a light that shines through the most ordinary woman – if she is happy and in love.

PAM BROWN, B.1928

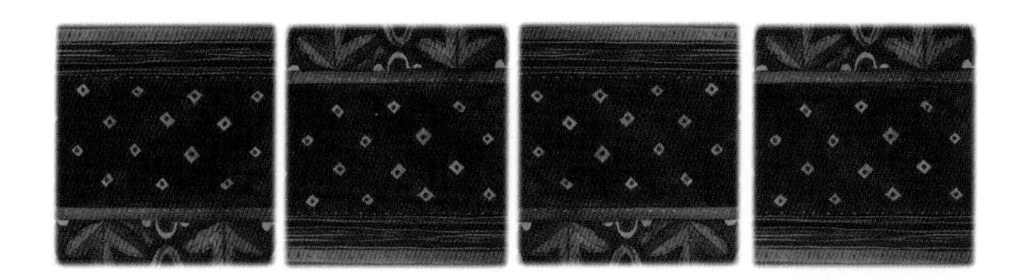

December 17

Falling in love is the greatest excitement of all.

PAM BROWN, B.1928

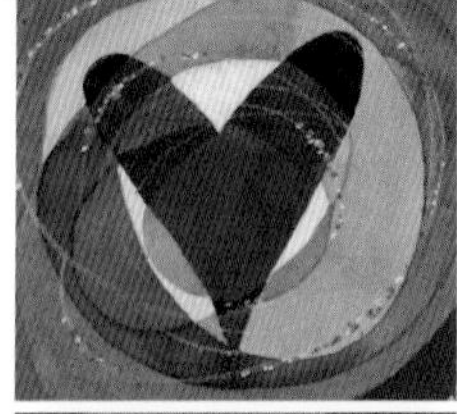

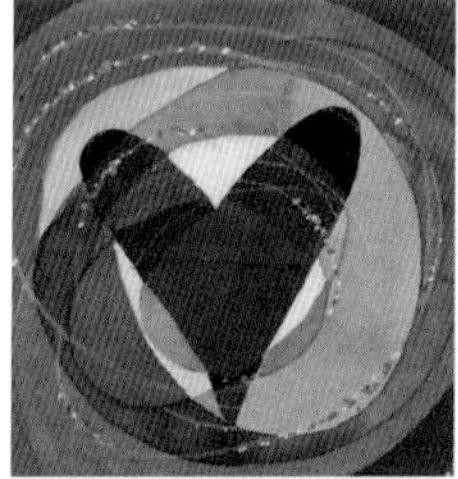

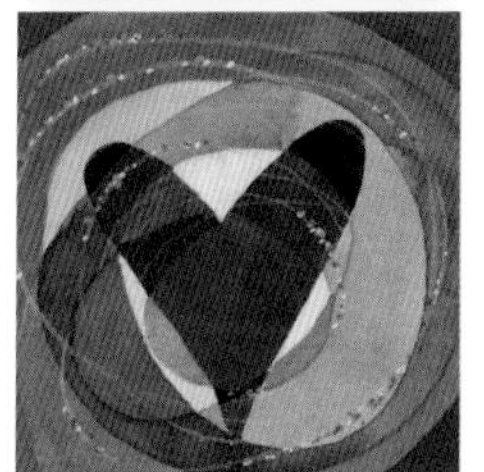

The disease of love has no physician.

SWAHILI LOVE POEM

December 16

Nothing can transform
one's life so dramatically
as love breaking through.
It is like the sun bursting
through dark clouds.
Suddenly everything
is amazingly different.

WENDY CRAIG

January 18

Gravity may hold us to the planet but love holds us together.

STUART & LINDA MACFARLANE

December 15

WINTER TWILIGHT
ON A WINDOW PANE
I WRITE YOUR NAME.

JAPANESE WISDOM

January 19

Riches take wings, comforts vanish,
hope withers away, but love stays with us.

LEWIS "LEW" WALLACE (1827-1905)

December 14

Love is the transforming power in our human nature. Love cries for life. Love fights for life.

SRI CHINMOY (1931-2007), FROM "THE WINGS OF JOY"

January 20

We never leave each other.
When does your mouth
say goodbye to your heart?

MARY TALL MOUNTAIN

December 13

Love cannot be regulated or sustained
by structures, rules or commitments.
It can only be sustained by
continuing acts of love which are marked
by gentleness, care, openness and trust.

FIONA CASTLE

January 21

The tender words we said to one another
are stored in the secret heart of heaven:
One day like rain they will fall and spread,
and our mystery will grow green over the world.

JALAL AL-DIN RUMI

December 12

How sad and bad
and mad it was –
But then,
how it was sweet!

ROBERT BROWNING (1812-1889)

January 22

Here's the scarf you left behind
holding the scent of you.
I press it to my face,
remembering.

CHARLOTTE GRAY, B.1937

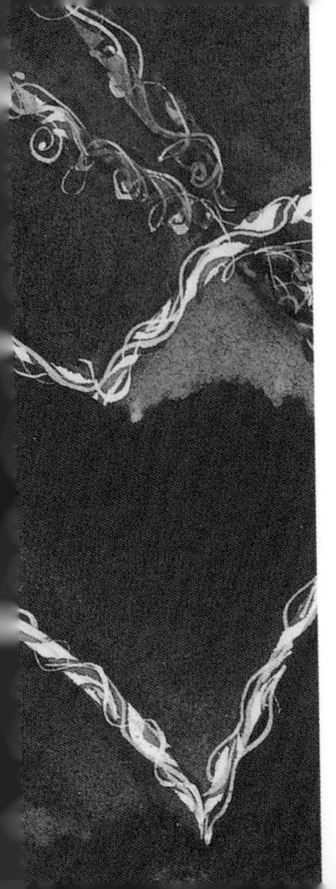

December 11

Love is not getting,
but giving.
Love is the best thing
in the world and the thing
that lives the longest.

HENRY VAN DYKE (1852-1933)

January 23

Without love, we are birds with broken wings.

MORRIE SCHWARTZ (1916-1995)

December 10

Love doesn't mean never having to say you are sorry. Love, at least lasting love, means being able to recognize when you need to say you are sorry.

CARMEN RENEE BERRY & TAMARA TRAEDER

January 24

Those who have never known the deep intimacy and hence the companionship of happy mutual love have missed the best thing that life has to give.

BERTRAND RUSSELL (1872-1970)

December 9

The love of ordinary people lights the world.

JENNY DE VRIES (1947-1991)

January 25

You are never too young
to fall in love
and never too old
to wish you had.

KERI NOBLE

Communication from a heart to a heart,
a soul to a soul, is worth more than a whole page,
a whole volume of books that could be written.

THE MUSKOGEE TRIBE

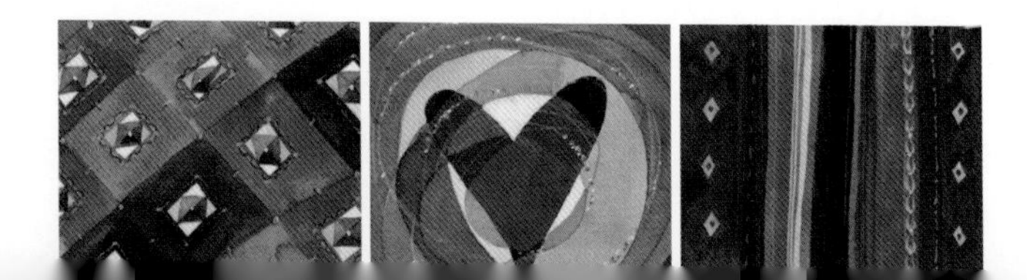

January 26

Everything that touches us,
me and you,
takes us together
like a violin's bow,
which draws one voice out
of two separate strings.

RAINER MARIA RILKE (1875-1926)

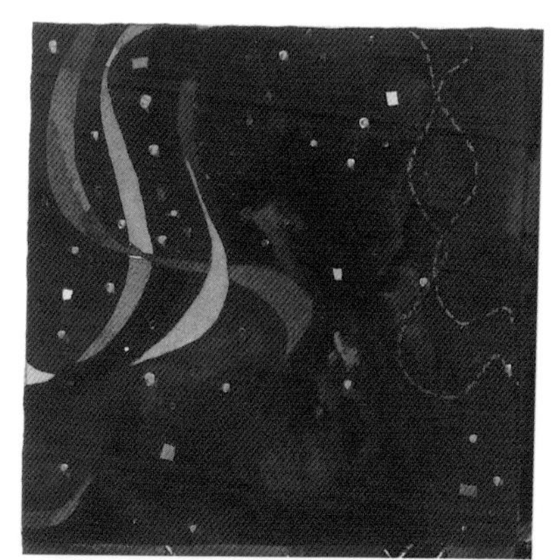

December 7

Love from one being to another can only be that two solitudes come nearer, recognize and protect and comfort each other.

MRS ELIZABETH COMBER (HAN SUYIN), B.1917

January 27

What comes
from the heart, touches
the heart.

DON SIBET

Intimacy in general terms
is a song of spirit inviting
two people to come and share
their spirit together. It is a song
that no one can resist.

SOBONFU SOMÉ

January 28

You can do anything and be anything, so long as it's with me.

DYLAN THOMAS (1914-1953),
IN A LETTER TO HIS WIFE-TO-BE CAITLIN MACNAMARA

December 5

I spread out the days before me – the days we have spent together – some bright as stars, some glowing with an opalescent magic, some cool as pebbles, some flashing with fire. What would they have been without you? Dates crossed off on a calendar.

MARION C. GARRETTY (1917-2005)

January 29

Being with you
is like walking on a very clear
morning – definitely
the sensation of belonging there.

E. B. WHITE (1899-1985)

December 4

Love is the common denominator that goes through all cultures and binds us together. Without it, we're lost.

BEARHEART (MUSKOGEE) (1918-2008)

January 30

When problems arise, we tend to forget about the strong foundation we have in our relationship. Remember where and when you and your partner felt the strongest, the closest, and the most intimate. When you are at the lowest point of your relationship, you can have that as a frame of reference.

SOBONFU SOMÉ

December 3

If you ever leave me,
I'm coming with you.

NAOMI JUDD, B.1946

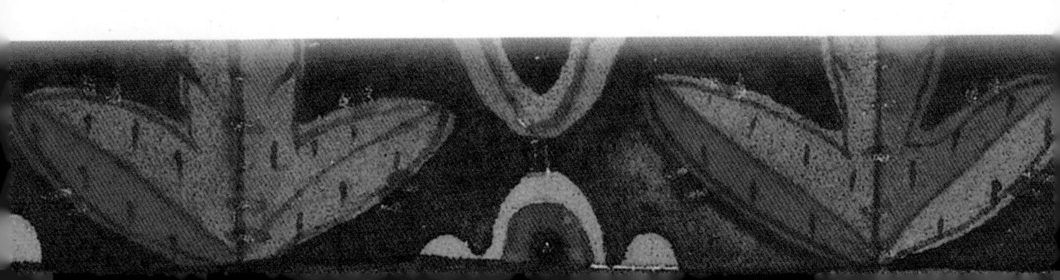

January 31

The entire sum of existence is the magic of being needed by just one person.

VI PUTNAM

December 2

You can't go out and earn love,
you can't buy it, borrow it
or even look for it.
You can look for a date and sex,
but not true love.
It doesn't work like that.

DAISY DOOLEY

February 1

When you remove love
and try to replace it
with monetary things,
you've got nothing.

JOHN PETERS

December 1

Your breath, like a spring shower makes my body tingle.
Your touch, like the summer sun makes my temperature soar.
Your voice, like an autumn breeze sets my heart a flutter.
Your kiss, like the winter snow sends shivers through my soul.

LINDA MACFARLANE, B.1953

February 2

Never above you. Never below you.
Always beside you.

WALTER WINCHELL (1897-1972)

November 30

Love is born with the pleasure
of looking at each other,
it is fed with the necessity of
seeing each other,
it is concluded with
the impossibility of separation!

JOSÉ MARTÍ Y PERÉZ, FROM "AMOR"

Love, whereby two people walk in different directions yet always remain side by side.

HUGH PRATHER (1938-2010)

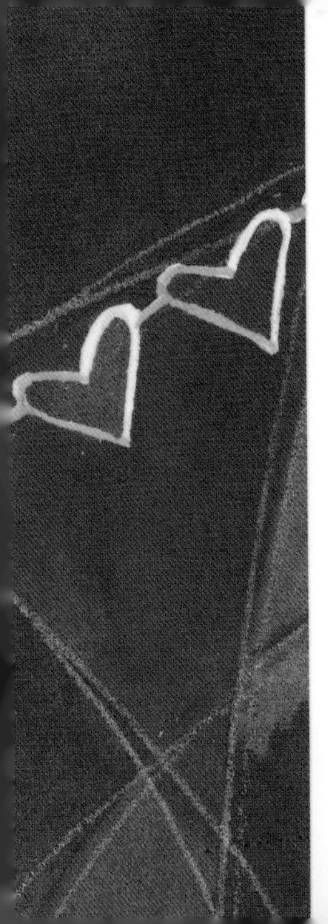

November 29

Congratulations!
You found each other!
Out of millions of lives – scattered across the planet – against all odds, all possibilities, all chance you found each other.
Never let each other go.

PAM BROWN, B.1928

February 4

Happiness is being snug abed with the person you love – and the rain lashing the window and drumming on the roof. Safe.

PAM BROWN, B.1928

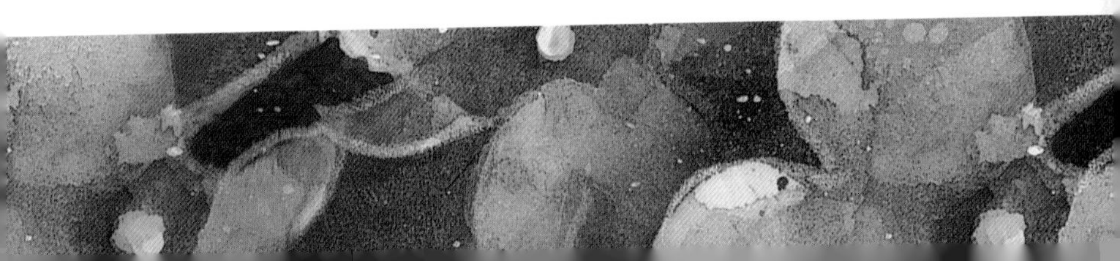

November 28

And true love holds with gentle hands
The hearts that it entwines.

AUTHOR UNKNOWN

February 5

It is the true season of Love
when we know that
we alone can love,
that no one could ever have
loved before us
and no one will ever Love
in the same way after us.

JOHANN WOLFGANG VON GOETHE
(1749-1832)

November 27

Whatever our souls are made of, his and mine are the same.

EMILY BRONTË (1818-1848)

February 6

He who defends with love will be secure.

LAO TZU (6TH CENTURY B.C.)

November 26

We treasure love. It quenches,
vexes, guides, and murders us.
It seeps into the mortar of all our days.
It feeds our passion, it fills our
fantasies, it inspires our art.

DIANE ACKERMAN

February 7

...if you love someone,
you need to be with them, close to them.
You need to be able to confide,
to laugh together.
It's just about as important as breathing.

ROSAMUNDE PILCHER, B.1924, FROM "SEPTEMBER"

We need to be loved and to love.

CHIEF DAN GEORGE (1899-1981)

Love has nothing to do with what
you are expecting to get – only what you are
expecting to give – which is everything.

KATHARINE HEPBURN (1907-2003)

November 24

I have spread my dreams under your feet;
Tread softly because you tread on my dreams.

WILLIAM BUTLER YEATS (1865-1939)

February 9

Don't ask me to leave you!
Let me go with you.
Wherever you go,
I will go; wherever you live
I will live.

OLD TESTAMENT

November 23

Love is, above all, the gift of oneself.

JEAN ANOUILH (1910-1987)

February 10

I am nearly mad about you as much as one can be mad; I cannot bring together two ideas that you do not interpose yourself between them. I can no longer think of anything but you.

STUART & LINDA MACFARLANE

November 22

We have made a home, gathered possessions, kept treasured souvenirs of all the joys we've shared.
All dear to me – yet if all were lost tomorrow and we were safe in each other's love – I'd mourn them only for a moment. All that is most precious can be held in arms.

PAM BROWN, B.1928

February 11

When two people
fall in love, each
comes in out of
the loneliness of exile,
home to the one house
of belonging.

JOHN O'DONOHUE

November 21

Love is trusting, accepting and believing, without guarantee. Love is patient and waits, but it's an active waiting, not a passive one. For it is continually offering itself in a mutual revealing, a mutual sharing. Love is spontaneous and craves expression through joy, through beauty, through truth, even through tears. Love lives the moment; it's neither lost in yesterday nor does it crave for tomorrow. Love is Now!

LEO BUSCAGLIA (1924-1998), FROM "LOVE"

February 12

Love is an act of
endless forgiveness,
a tender look
which becomes a habit.

PETER USTINOV (1921-2004)

November 20

Love is like playing the piano.
First you must learn to play by the rules,
then you must forget the rules and play
from your heart.

AUTHOR UNKNOWN

February 13

Time is too slow for those
who wait, too swift for
those who fear, too long
for those who grieve,
too short for those who rejoice,
but for those who love,
time is eternity.

HENRY VAN DYKE (1852-1933)

Man and woman are two locked caskets, of which each contains the key.

ISAK DINESEN (1885-1962)

February 14

My heart has made its
mind up
And I'm afraid it's you.

WENDY COPE, B.1945, FROM "VALENTINE"

November 18

You make me glad to be alive.

STUART & LINDA MACFARLANE

February 15

Security is when I'm very much in love with somebody extraordinary who loves me back.

SHELLEY WINTERS (1920-2006)

November 17

Love is comfort in sadness, quietness in tumult, rest in weariness, hope in despair.

MARION C. GARRETTY (1917-2005)

February 16

Love never dies. It may look different, take on different shapes, ebb, flow, flicker, and blaze, but it is the one thing in this world that never, ever dies.

KYLA MERWIN

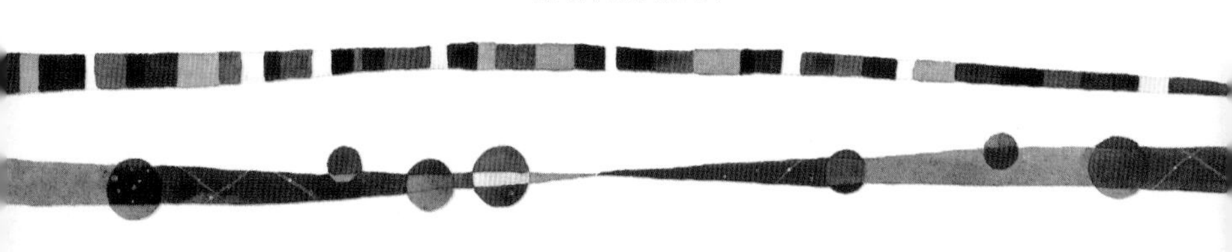

November 16

A good marriage is passion and monotony, practicalities, magic, talk and tears and laughter. And at the core lies a secret place. A place of trust and love and deep content.

PAM BROWN, B.1928

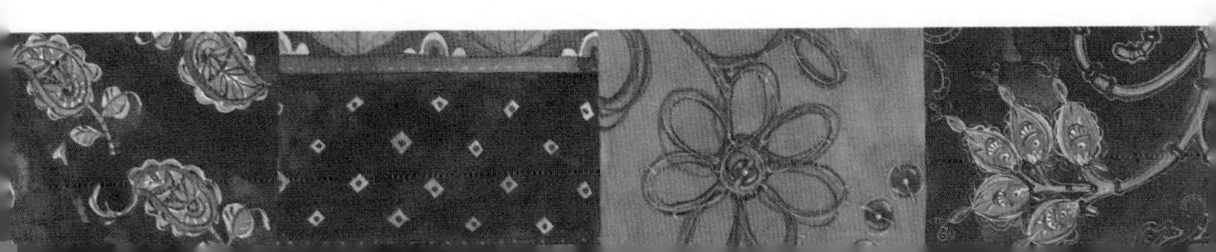

February 17

MY LIFETIME LISTENS TO YOURS.

MURIEL RUKEYSER (1913-1980)

November 15

Nothing is more important to human beings than to be loved.

CELIA BOWRING

February 18

Love is supposed to start with bells ringing and go downhill from there. But it was the opposite for me. There's an intense connection between us, and as we stayed together, the bells rang louder.

LISA NIEMI

November 14

Being in love is the excitement of the moment, that sharp blade of exhilaration which cleaves through the seconds and makes the world sparkle.

STEVE BOWKETT

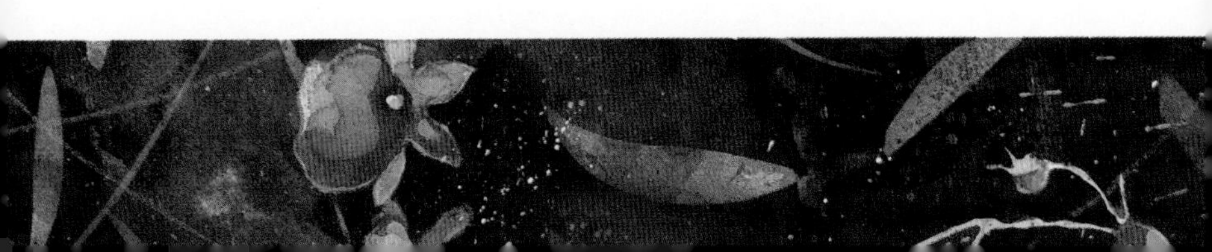

February 19

For all the little, unexpected surprises.
For all the enduring kindness – thank you.

PAM BROWN, B.1928

November 13

Love…can only be given and received.
It cannot be taken.

ORIAH MOUNTAIN DREAMER

February 20

The smallest whisper of love can restore confidence and sureness.

JOHN O'DONOHUE

November 12

TO BE LOVED IS THE TRIUMPH OF LIVING.

ANTHONY QUINN (1915-2001), FROM "ONE MAN TANGO"

February 21

To fear love is to fear life;
and those that fear life
are already three parts dead.

BERTRAND RUSSELL (1872-1970)

There are no limits to love.

MICHAEL CAINE, B.1933, FROM "WHAT'S IT ALL ABOUT?"

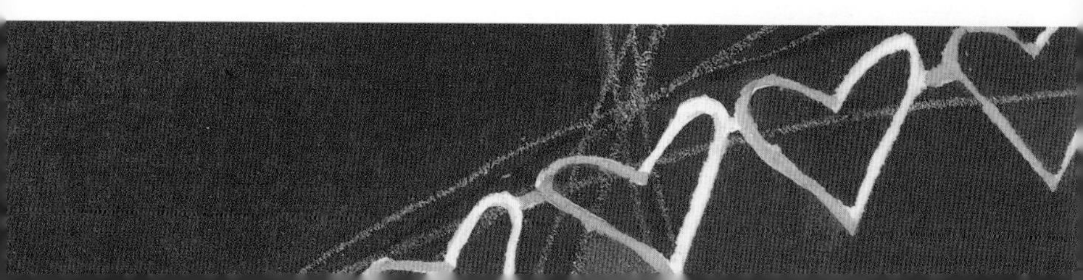

February 22

The first duty of love is to listen.

PAUL TILLICH (1886-1965)

November 10

A very ordinary couple
in a very ordinary house –
but what an extraordinary love
we share.

CLARA ORTEGA, B.1955

February 23

I want to be your friend
forever and ever.
When the hills are all flat and the rivers
are all dry, when the trees blossom
in winter and the snow falls in summer,
when heaven and earth mix –
not till then will I part from you.

THE YÜEH-FU

November 9

Love distracts
one from the tidiest plans,
the narrowest course,
the clearest goals.

DIANE ACKERMAN

February 24

The quiet thoughts
of two people a long time in love
touch lightly like birds nesting in
each other's warmth. You will
know them by their laughter....

HUGH PRATHER (1938-2010)

November 8

Union gives strength.

AESOP, FROM "THE BUNDLE OF STICKS"

February 25

Love may have its ups and downs – but it's better to be in than out.

STUART & LINDA MACFARLANE

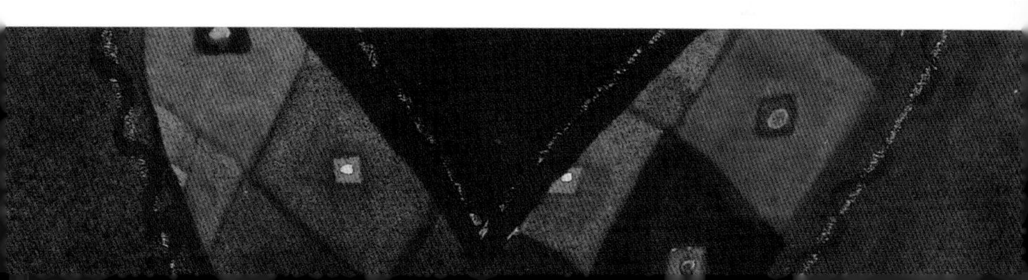

November 7

One hour of right-down love
Is worth an age of dully living on.

APHRA BEHN (1640-1689)

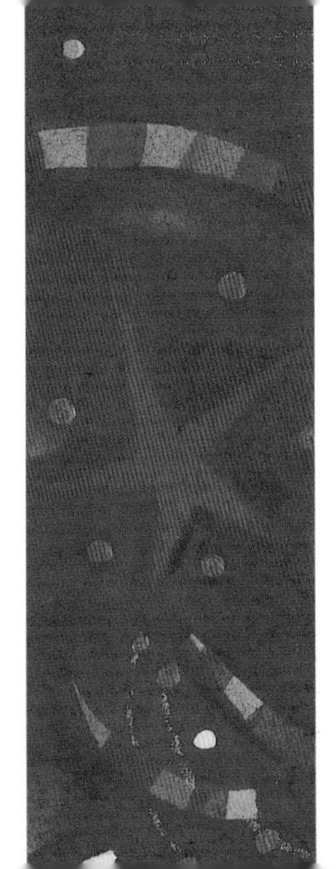

February 26

A star is shining in my heart,
My dreams have wings
that touch the sky,
I'd marry you a thousand times –
I'll love you till the day I die.

MARION SCHOEBERLEIN

November 6

Love is knowing someone else cares.

AUTHOR UNKNOWN

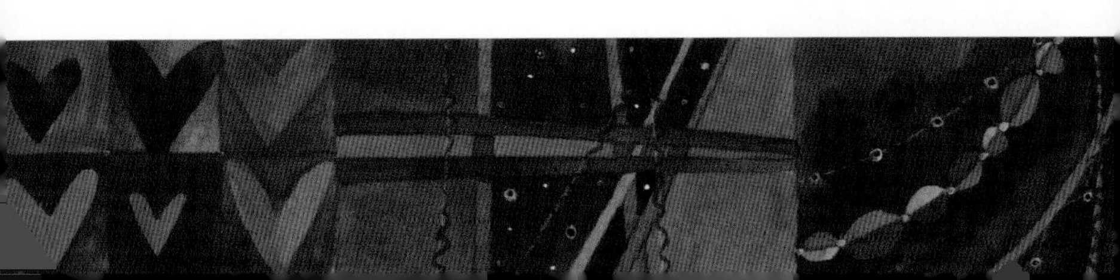

February 27

...when Love speaks,
the voice of all the gods
make heaven drowsy
with the harmony.

WILLIAM SHAKESPEARE (1564-1616),
FROM "LOVE'S LABOURS LOST"

November 5

Life is the first gift,
love is the second,
and understanding the third.

MARGE PIERCY, B.1936

All of our experiences in life
make us not less valuable,
but more valuable,
not less able to love,
but more able to love.

JOANNA CAMPBELL SLAN

November 4

LOVE is a game that two can play and both win.

EVA GABOR (1919-1995)

March 1

The wind whispering secrets to the trees,
The snowflakes floating on crisp clear air.
Their beauty would be lost,
Their enchantment stolen,
Should I ever have to live without your love.

STUART & LINDA MACFARLANE

November 3

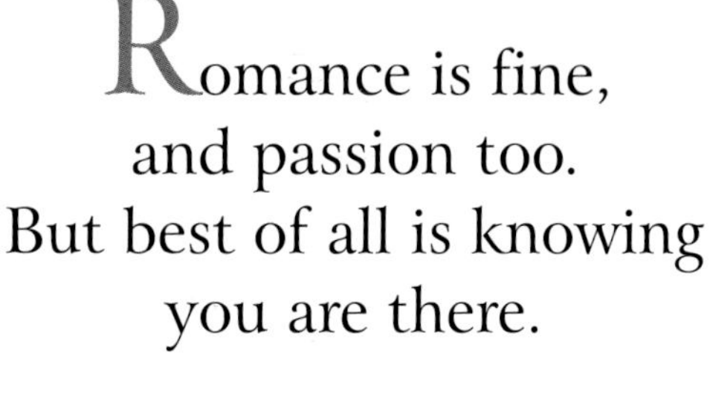

Romance is fine,
and passion too.
But best of all is knowing
you are there.

JENNY DE VRIES (1947-1991)

March 2

Love is a net where hearts are caught like fish.

SUFI SAYING

November 2

Until the stars fall from the sky,
Until the seas melt away,
I shall always love you.

LINDA MACFARLANE, B.1953

March 3

Love doesn't just sit there
like a stone;
it has to be made,
like bread, remade
all the time, made new.

URSULA K. LE GUIN

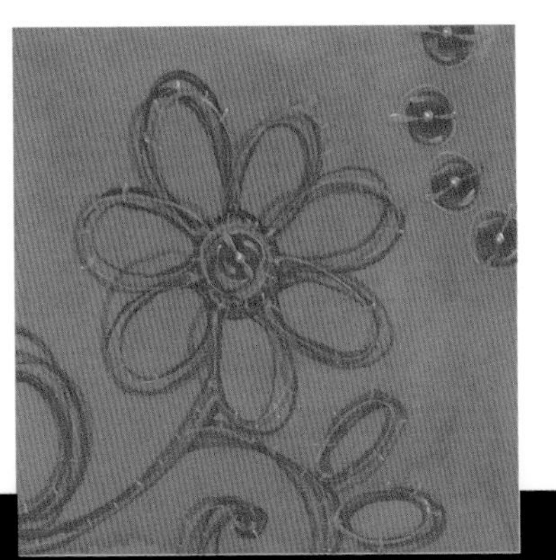

November 1

Only when one is open to receive and absorb love can it occur.

JOAN ANDERSON, FROM "A YEAR BY THE SEA"

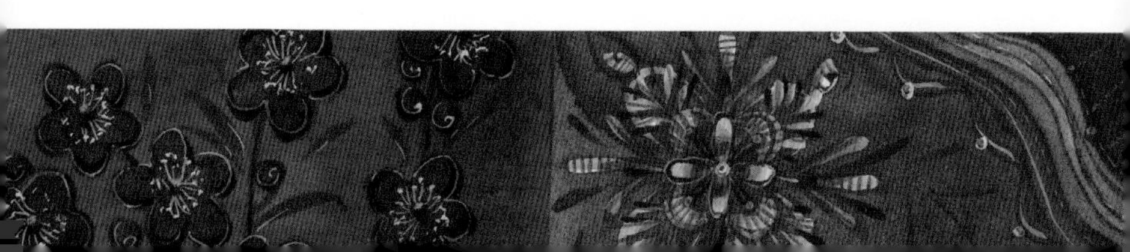

Saying "I love you" is a conversation, not a message.

DOUGLAS STONE

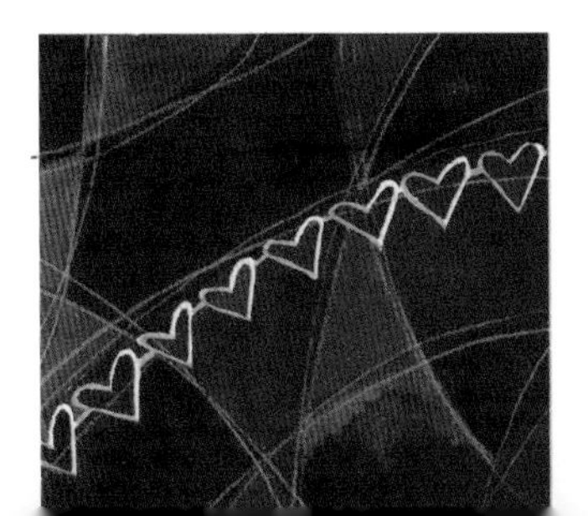

October 31

...were I crowned the most
imperial monarch,
Thereof most trustworthy,
were I the fairest youth
That ever made eye swerve,
had force and knowledge
More than was ever man's
I would not prize them
Without her love.

WILLIAM SHAKESPEARE (1564-1616),
FROM "THE WINTER'S TALE"

ALL LOVE IS SWEET,
GIVEN OR RETURNED.

PERCY BYSSHE SHELLEY
(1792-1822)

October 30

This is the life I love. For I'm with you.
You are the root of all I do, and am.

PAM BROWN, B.1928

March 6

In the rich tapestry of life it is the bright threads of love that fashion the scenes of happiness.

STUART & LINDA MACFARLANE

Love turns one person into two and two into one.

ISAAC ABARBANEL

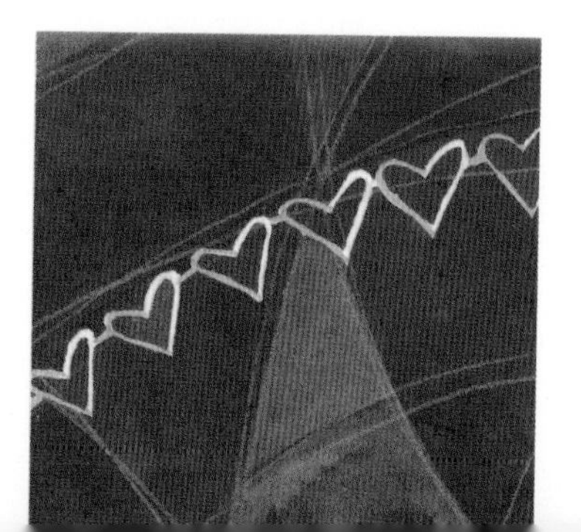

March 7

You live
that you may learn to love.
You love
that you may learn to live.
No other lesson
is required of us.

MIKHAIL NAIMY (1889-1988)

October 28

To love and to be loved
is the greatest happiness of existence.

SYDNEY SMITH (1771-1845)

What is yours is mine,
and all mine is yours.

PLAUTUS (c.254-184 B.C.)

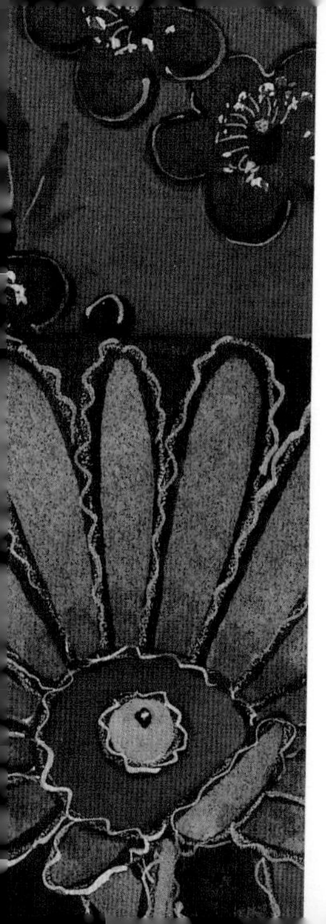

October 27

In love,
Dare to dream,
For two shape a future,
Filled with happiness,
Beyond imagination.

STUART & LINDA MACFARLANE

In a full heart
there is room for everything,
and in an empty heart
there is room for nothing.

ANTONIO PORCHIA

October 26

Without love
our life is a ship
without a rudder...
like a body
without a soul.

SHOLEM ALEICHEM (1859-1916)

Your task is not to seek for love,
but merely to seek
and find all the barriers within yourself
that you have built against it.

JALAL AL-DIN RUMI

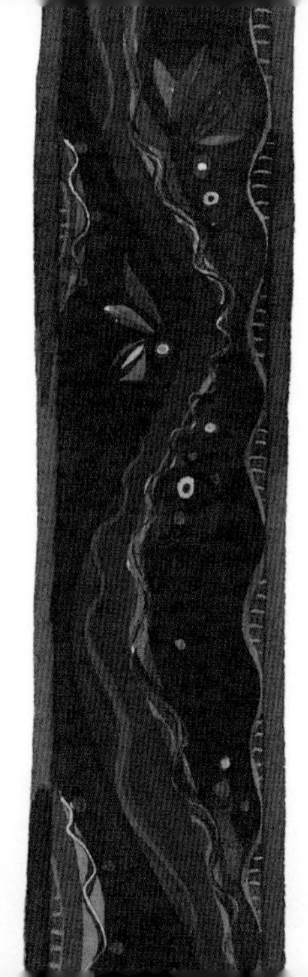

October 25

Love changes things;
it is the most powerful force
in the world. A person motivated
by love is the most potent force
there is. There are other forces
that are potent, such as hatred.
But love is a greater force.

MILLARD FULLER

March 11

And when we kiss, a current surges, heart to heart, carrying all my love to him and all his love to me.

LINDA MACFARLANE, B.1953

A heart enlightened by love is more precious than all of the diamonds and gold in the world.

MUHAMMAD ALI, B.1942

March 12

Age does not protect you
from love.
But love, to some extent,
protects you from age.

JEANNE MOREAU, B.1928

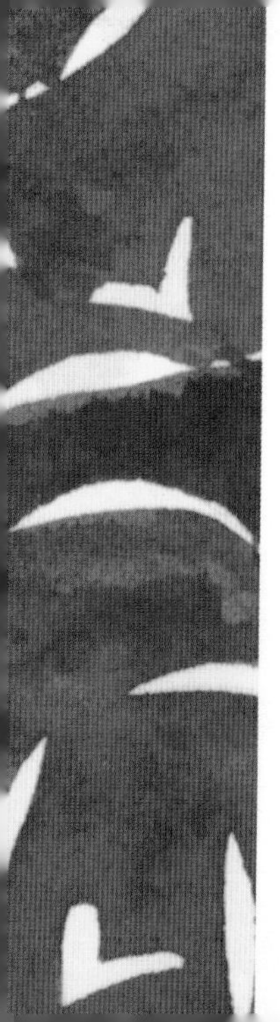

October 23

The countless generations
Like Autumn leaves go by:
Love only is eternal,
Love only does not die....

HARRY KEMP, FROM "THE PASSING FLOWER"

To love and be loved is to feel the sun from both sides.

DAVID VISCOTT (1938-1996)

Thank you for believing I'm special.

PAM BROWN, B.1928

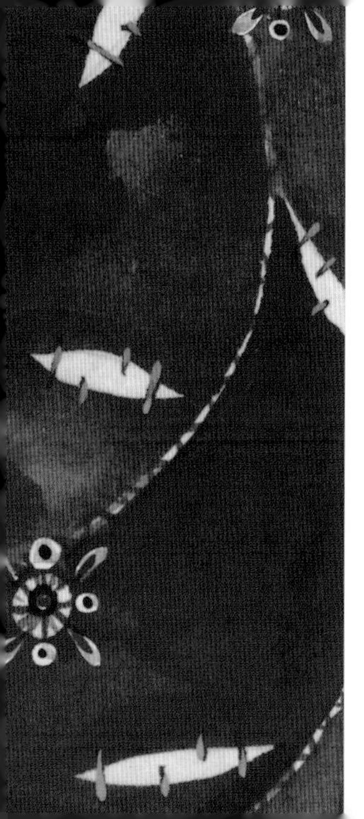

March 14

Anything, everything,
little or big becomes
an adventure when
the right person shares it.

KATHLEEN NORRIS (1880-1966)

October 21

There is nothing more lovely
in life than the union of
two people whose love
for one another has grown
through the years
from the small acorn of passion
to a great rooted tree.

VITA SACKVILLE-WEST (1892-1962)

Love is never elusive.
In all its permutations, love surrounds us
in the world, whether
we are accepting of it or not.

SIDNEY POITIER, B.1927

October 20

Love is when
the desire to be desired
takes you so badly
that you feel
you could die of it.

HENRI DE TOULOUSE-LAUTREC
(1864-1901)

Loving affection for living beings is the water with which to irrigate the field of the mind and make it fertile.

GESHE SONAM RINCHEN, FROM "THE BODHISATTVA VOW"

 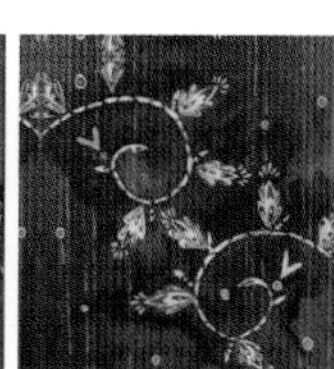 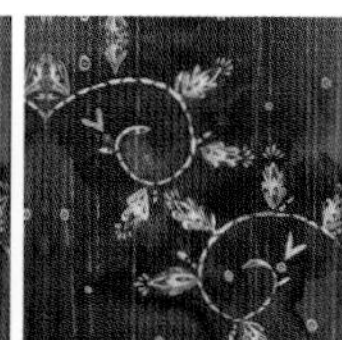 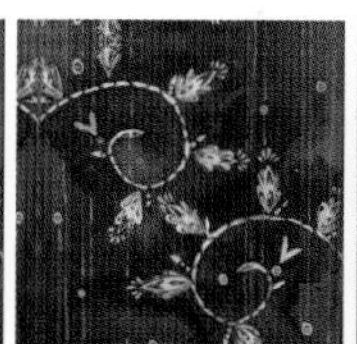 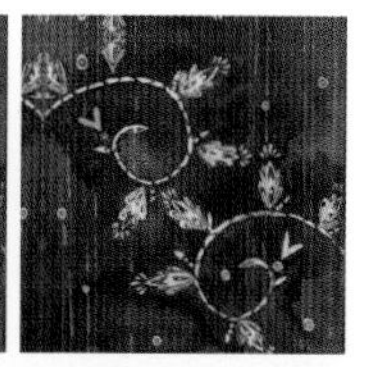

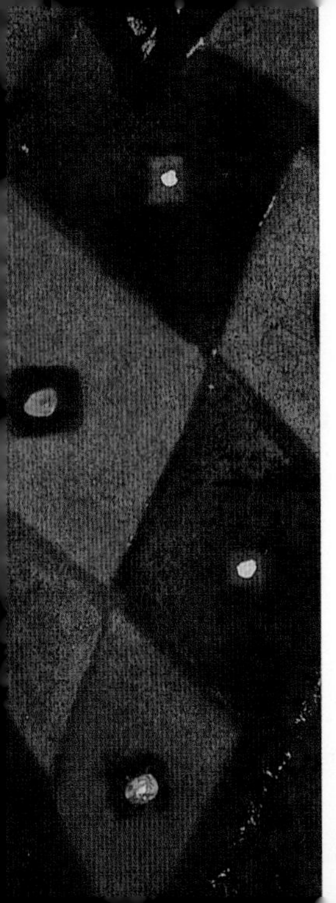

October 19

All those millions of lives
– and yet we found one another.

PAM BROWN, B.1928

BETWEEN A MAN
AND HIS WIFE
NOTHING OUGHT
TO RULE
BUT LOVE.

WILLIAM PENN (1644-1718)

October 18

Without love there is no life.

THOMAS MASARYK

March 18

Affection is a coal that must be cooled,
Else, suffered, it will set the heart on fire.
The sea hath bounds,
but deep desire hath none.

WILLIAM SHAKESPEARE (1564-1616),
FROM "VENUS AND ADONIS"

October 17

One word frees us of all the weight and pain of life:
The word is "love."

SOPHOCLES (496-406 B.C.)

March 19

Come what may as long as you live,
it is day.
And if I in the world must roam,
Wherever you are that is home.
When your loving voice I hear
The future's shadows disappear.

THEODOR STORM (1817-1888)

October 16

Love with all your heart.
Listen with all your soul.

STUART & LINDA MACFARLANE

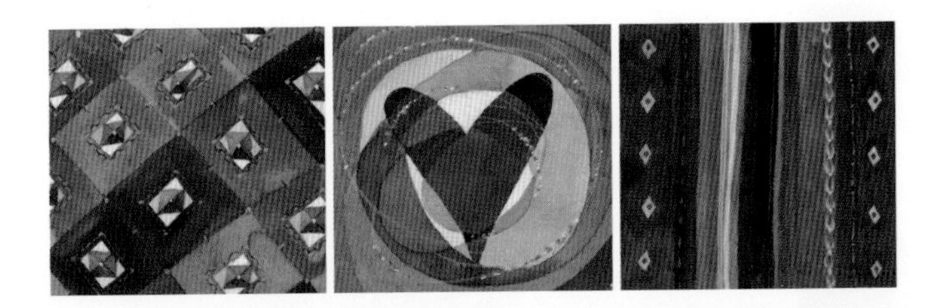

March 20

Familiar acts are beautiful through love.

PERCY BYSSHE SHELLEY (1792-1822), FROM "PROMETHEUS UNBOUND"

Where love is concerned, too much is not ever enough!

PIERRE AUGUSTIN CARON DE BEAUMARCHAIS
(1732-1799)

March 21

To love means to say:
it is good that you are you,
it is very good.

LADISLAAUS BOROS (1927-1981)

When love enters into people whose hearts are not withered, it makes them want to love everyone.

SIMONE DE BEAUVOIR,
FROM "AFTER THE WAR: FORCE OF CIRCUMSTANCE"

Even the most ordinary day
is made special by your love.

PAM BROWN, B.1928

October 13

A life without any love is no life at all.

KATHRYN FLETT

Sally has a smile I would accept as my last view of earth.

WALLACE STEGNER (1909-1993)

October 12

Love is like young rice:
transplanted, still it grows.

MADAGASCAN LOVE QUOTATION

Love doesn't attempt to bind, ensnare, capture.
It is light, free of the burden of attachments.
Love asks nothing, is fulfilled in itself.
When love is there, nothing remains to be done.

VIMALA THAKAR

October 11

It's easy to forget
that what people need most
in the world cannot
be satisfied by material
things alone.
What they ask of us is love.

FROM "THE FRIENDSHIP BOOK
OF FRANCIS GAY"

March 25

Love cures people,
both the ones who give it,
and the ones
who receive it.

KARL MENNINGER (1893-1990)

October 10

Every day I know you better.
Every day I love you more.

PAM BROWN, B.1928

March 26

I love you soulfully
and bodyfully,
properly and improperly,
every way that a woman
can be loved.

GEORGE BERNARD SHAW
(1856-1950),
TO ELLEN TERRY

October 9

All that I love loses half its pleasure
if you are not there to share it.

CLARA ORTEGA, B.1955

In love all of life's contradictions dissolve and disappear. Only in love are unity and duality not in conflict.

RABINDRANATH TAGORE (1861-1941)

October 8

You are the future
of my past,
the present of my always,
the forever of my now.

CHARLES GHIGNA

March 28

My bounty is as boundless as the sea,
My love as deep; the more I give to thee
The more I have, for both are infinite.

WILLIAM SHAKESPEARE (1564-1616),
FROM "ROMEO AND JULIET"

October 7

Women wish to be loved without a why or a wherefore; not because they are pretty, or good, or well-bred, or graceful, or intelligent, but because they are themselves.

HENRI FRÉDÉRIC AMIEL (1821-1881)

Wherever you are, I am there also.

LUDWIG VAN BEETHOVEN (1770-1827)

October 6

Love blossoms when there is just the right amount of tenderness combined with a long leash.

JOAN ANDERSON, FROM "A YEAR BY THE SEA"

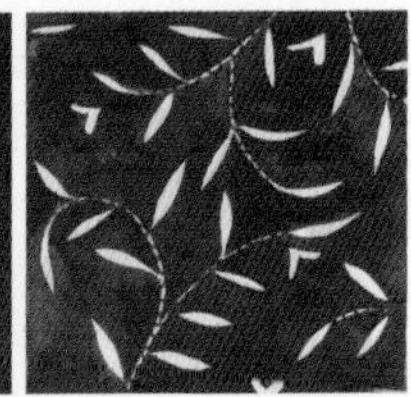

Most certain and more sure – the heartbeat
that marks time to all I do – my second self
and yet uniquely you. Nothing can overwhelm me
utterly, so long as you are here.
Distance can never separate us.
Time can only bring us closer.

PAM BROWN, B.1928

He poured so gently and naturally
into my life like batter into a bowl of batter.
Honey into a jar of honey.
The clearest water sinking into sand.

JUSTINE SYDNEY

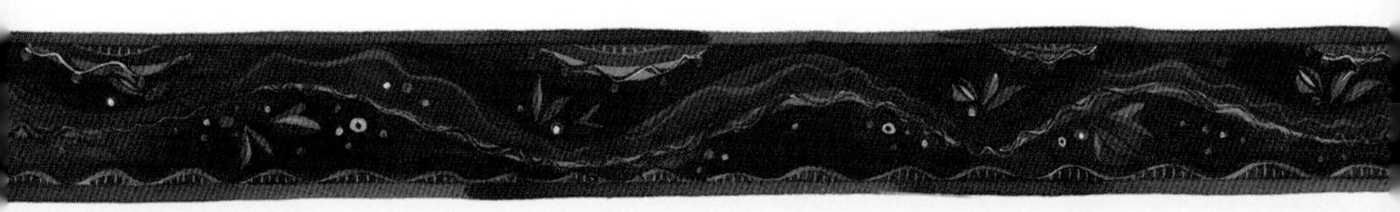

March 31

What happiness to be beloved;
and O, what bliss, ye gods, to love!

JOHANN WOLFGANG VON GOETHE (1749-1832)

October 4

...No one knows how it is that with one glance a boy can break through into a girl's heart.

NAPOLEON BONAPARTE

April 1

If this is love... can I have seconds?

STUART & LINDA MACFARLANE

October 3

Love is a force more formidable
than any other. It is invisible –
it cannot be seen or measured – yet is
powerful enough to transform you
in a moment, and offer you more joy than
any material possession ever could.

BARBARA DE ANGELIS

April 2

. . . Still with me

So, either by thy picture or my love,
Thyself away thou art present still with me;
For thou not farther than my thoughts canst move,
And I am still with them, and they with thee. . . .

WILLIAM SHAKESPEARE (1564-1616), FROM "SONNET 47"

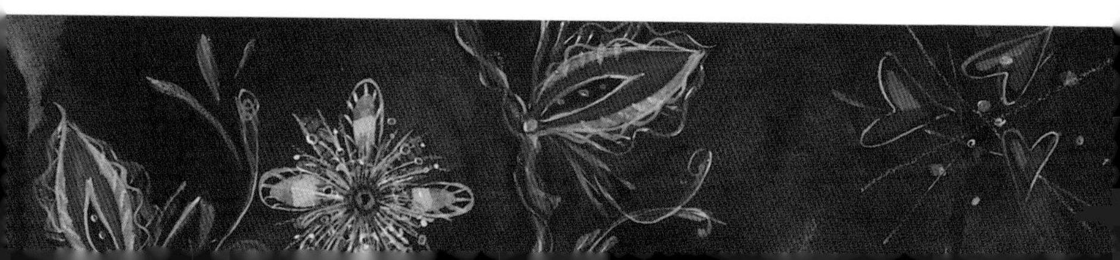

October 2

Love is a peasant emotion
and thrives as well in stables
as in palaces.
Of all the errands life seems
to be running,
of all the mysteries
that enchant us,
love is my favorite.

DIANE ACKERMAN

April 3

Those who love deeply never grow old;
they may die of old age, but they die young.

SIR ARTHUR WING PINERO (1855-1934)

October 1

Carry me off into the blue skies of tender loves, roll me in dark clouds, trample me with your thunderstorms, break me in your angry rages. But love me, my adored lover.

SARAH BERNHARDT (1844-1923), TO JEAN RICHEPIN

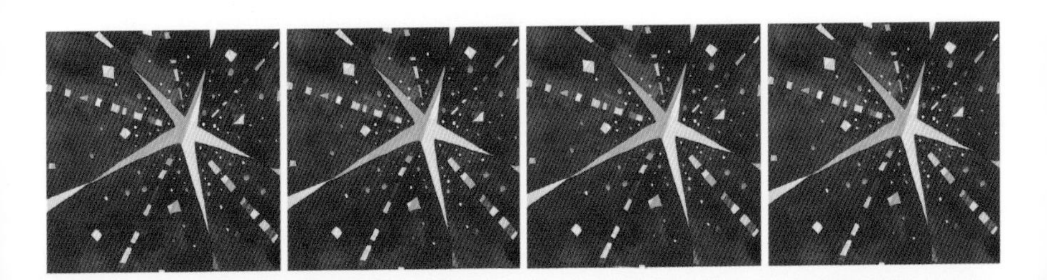

April 4

Of all forms of caution, caution in love is perhaps the most fatal to true happiness.

BERTRAND RUSSELL (1872-1970)

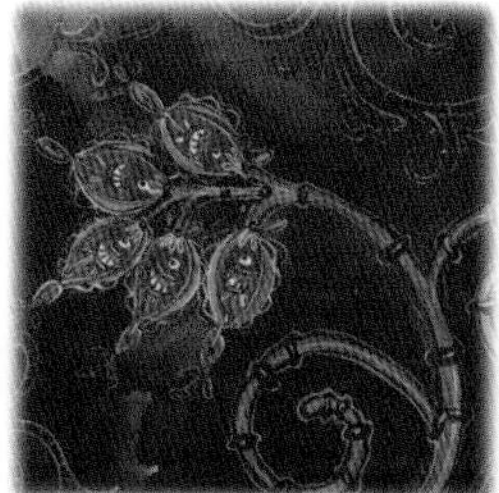

September 30

Love like yours creates a world
within a world.
A refuge. Somewhere to call home.

PAM BROWN, B.1928

When you are touched by love,
it reaches down into your deepest fibre.
When you are loved, your heart rushes forth
in the joy of the dance of life.
Love awakens the youthfulness of the heart.

JOHN O'DONOHUE

September 29

Love is a taste of paradise.

SHOLEM ALEICHEM (1859-1916)

April 6

Love is a wonderful thing. It is more precious than emeralds, and dearer than fine opals. Pearls and pomegranates cannot buy it, nor is it set forth in the market-place. It may not be purchased of the merchants, nor can it be weighed out in the balance for gold.

OSCAR WILDE (1854-1900)

September 28

To see her is to love her,
and love but her forever,
for nature made her what she is,
and ne'er made another!

ROBERT BURNS (1759-1796)

7

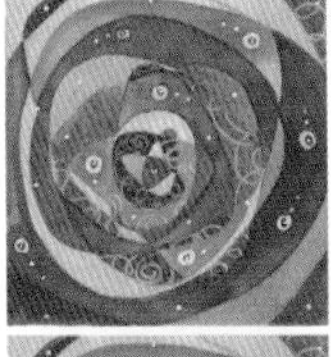

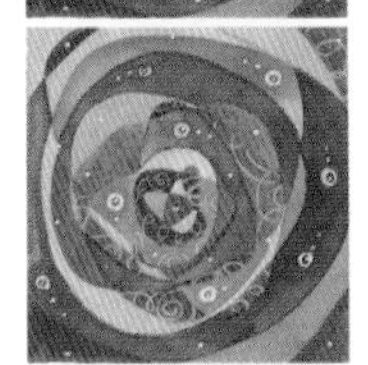

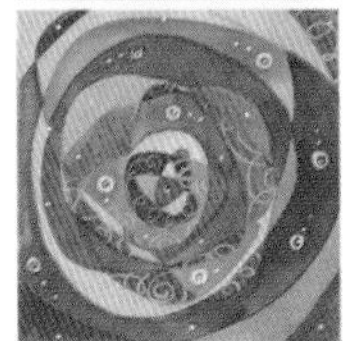

ALONE IN A CROWD
I CAN FEEL ISOLATED IN SECRET JOY
JUST THINKING OF HIM.

N. PAYNE

September 27

That which is loved is always beautiful.

NORWEGIAN PROVERB

April 8

There is a comfort in the strength of love;
Twill make a thing endurable, which else
Would overset the brain, or break the heart.

WILLIAM WORDSWORTH (1770-1850)

September 26

No one who has ever brought up a child can doubt for a moment that love is literally the life-giving fluid of human existence.

DR. SMILEY BLANTON

April 9

Love is totally unpredictable.
You never know where it is going to turn up
and in what form. And you can never have
enough of it. Love is a state of grace.

KATHY LETTE, B.1958

September 25

As selfishness and complaint pervert and cloud the mind, so love with its joys clears and sharpens the vision.

HELEN KELLER (1880-1968)

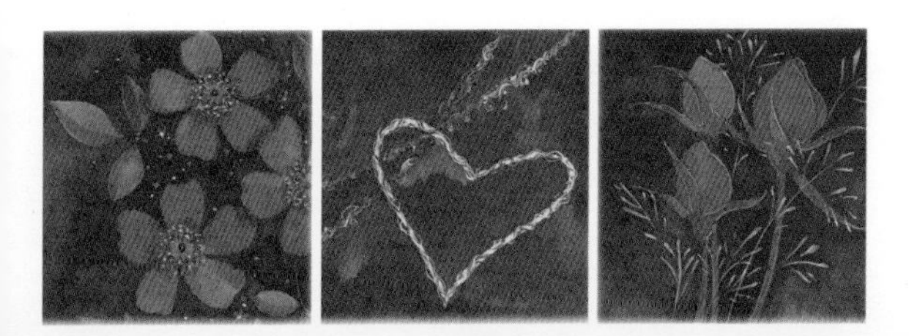

10

The ultimate test of a relationship is to disagree but to hold hands.

ALEXANDRA PENNEY

September 24

Love, you know, is strangely whimsical,
containing affronts, jabs, parleys, wars
then peace again. Now, for you to ask advice to
love by, is as if you ask advice to run mad by.

TERENCE (c.192-157 B.C.)

What's mine is yours, and what is yours is mine.

WILLIAM SHAKESPEARE (1564-1616), FROM "MEASURE FOR MEASURE"

September 23

You smile in passing, touch my shoulder.
I walk with you in the garden,
sharing the last of the light,
the flickering of bats, the scent of roses.
We are at home in quietness.
Passion and the everyday flow
from each other – equal expressions
of our love.

CHARLOTTE GRAY, B.1937

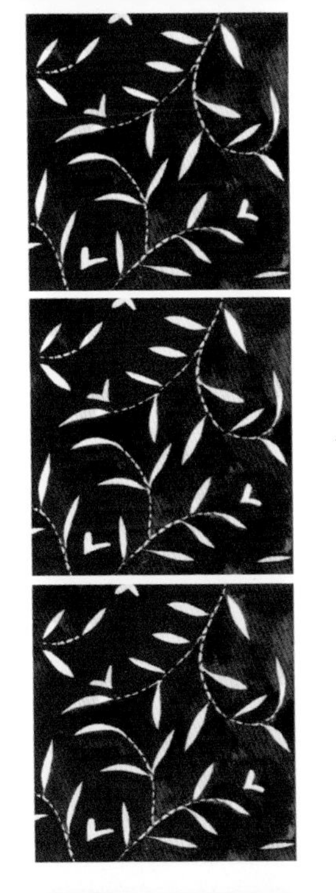

April 12

The friendship between us,
the mutual confidence, the delights
of the heart, the enchantment of
the soul, these things do not perish
and can never be destroyed.
I shall love you until I die.

VOLTAIRE (FRANÇOIS-MARIE AROUET)
(1694-1778), TO MME. DENIS

September 22

Wherever you're beside me... that's my home.

BILLY JOEL, B.1949

13

In love, when one person takes a knock it is the other who sheds the tears.

STUART & LINDA MACFARLANE

September 21

Nothing in this world is more
powerful than love. Not money,
greed, hate or passion.
Words cannot describe it.
Poets and writers try.
They can't because it is different
for each of us.

AUTHOR UNKNOWN

You are washed with the whitest fire of life
– when you take a woman
you love – and understand.

D. H. LAWRENCE (1885-1930)

September 20

I love you because
you have done more
than any creed could have done
to make me good,
and more than any fate
could have done to make
me happy.

ROY CROFT (1907-1973)

15

We take our own magic with us you and I.

PAM BROWN, B.1928

September 19

Don't you think I was made for you? I feel like you had me ordered – and I was delivered to you – to be worn – I want you to wear me, like a watch-charm or a buttonhole bouquet – to the world.

ZELDA FITZGERALD (1900-1948)

April 16

Love is something sent from Heaven to worry the hell out of you.

DOLLY PARTON

September 18

Once again last night you would not let me sleep. Before I went to sleep I moved over and made room for you and tried to imagine you there so soft and warm and smooth. I put out a hand and was disappointed.

BOB GRAFTON, TO HIS FUTURE WIFE DOT

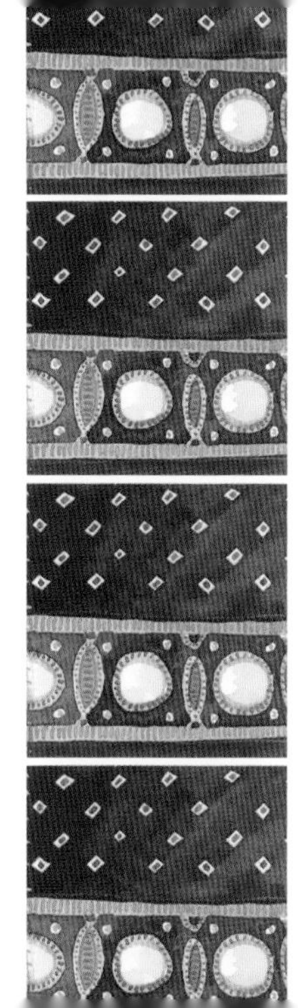

17

The most beautiful word
in any language
is our own name spoken to us
with love by somebody we love.

JEFFREY MASSON

September 17

I have found comfort
in your arms
Courage in weakness
Hope in despair
Laughter Love.

PAM BROWN, B.1928

April 18

Love comforteth, like sunshine after rain,
Love's gentle spring doth always fresh remain.

WILLIAM SHAKESPEARE (1564-1616),
FROM "VENUS AND ADONIS"

September 16

Loving one another is our only reason for being.

DOLLY PARTON

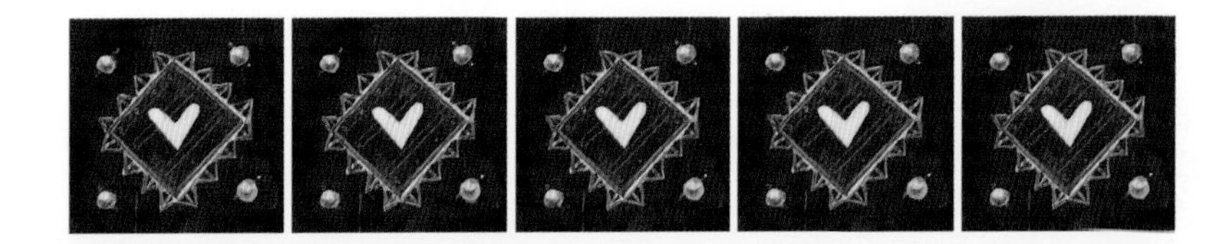

April 19

Whenever you share love with another, you'll notice the peace that comes to you and to them.

MOTHER TERESA (1910-1997)

September 15

Wherever I am,
My heart is with you, my love.
The river can not keep me from you.
In my mind's eye,
I see always you, my love.
Nothing can divide us, one from one.
My heart sings for you, my only love.

ZULU LOVE POEM

April 20

Keep love in your heart.
The consciousness of loving
and being loved brings a warmth
and richness to life that nothing
else can bring.

OSCAR WILDE (1854-1900)

September 14

THANK YOU FOR BEING HERE.
THANK YOU FOR EVERYTHING.

MAYA PATEL, B.1943

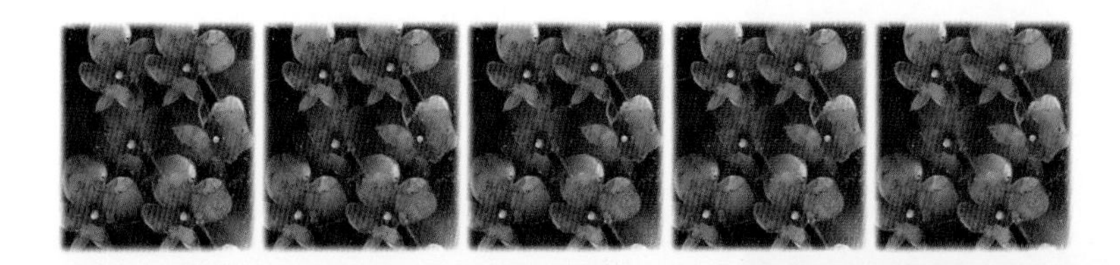

April 21

There is a way from
your heart to mine
and my heart knows it.

JALAL AL-DIN RUMI

September 13

Love, I've come to understand,
is more than three words mumbled
before bedtime.
Love is sustained by action,
a pattern of devotion in the things
we do for each other every day.

NICHOLAS SPARKS

April 22

Love is not merely the indulgence of one's personal taste buds, it is also the delight in indulging another's.

LAURIE LEE (1914-1997)

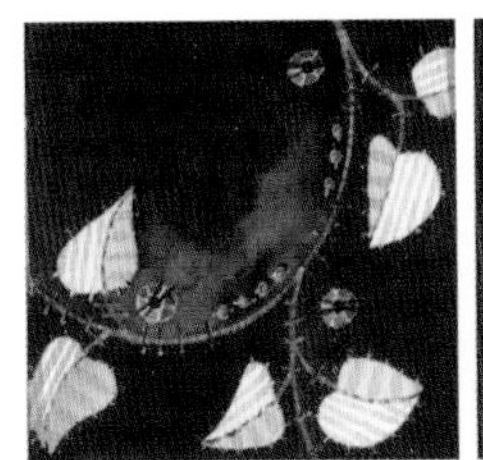
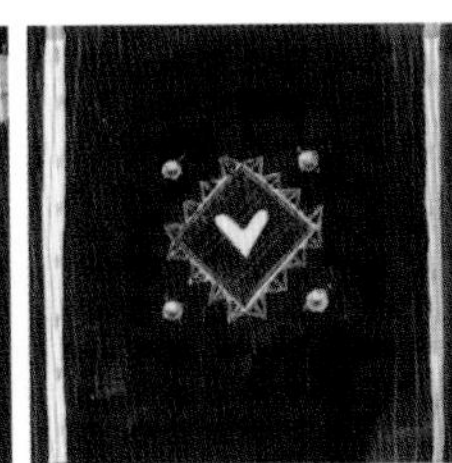

September 12

I bless you. I kiss and caress every tenderly beloved place and gaze into your deep, sweet eyes which long ago conquered me completely.

TSARITSA ALEXANDRA

April 23

What is important
is that one is capable of love.
It is perhaps the only
glimpse we are permitted
of eternity.

HELEN HAYES (1900-1993)

September 11

One look and my soul sings, one word and my heart flutters. One touch and my whole body thrills with delight.

LINDA MACFARLANE, B.1953

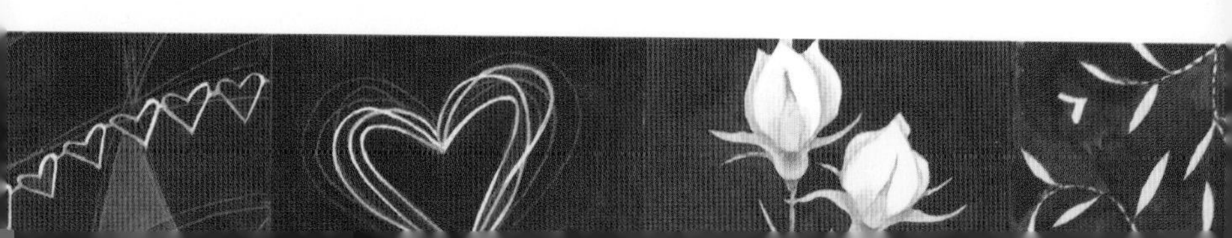

Love is a settled heart
and a big heart.
Love encompasses everything
inside of you.

STUART WILDE

September 10

I love you when you laugh so much
you slither off the chair.
When you sleep all sprawled and limp
like a little child.

PAM BROWN, B.1928

The most important thing in life is to learn how to give out love, and to let it come in.

MORRIE SCHWARTZ (1916-1995)

Unconditional love is the most precious gift we can give. Being forgiven for the past is the most precious gift we can receive.

SARAH J. VOGT

April 26

Woman, in your laughter you have the music of the fountain of life.

RABINDRANATH TAGORE (1861-1941)

September 8

There is nothing more precious in this world than the feeling of being wanted.

DIANA DORS (1931-1984)

Love is the strongest of nature's forces – able to bring joy even out of tragedy.

STUART & LINDA MACFARLANE

September 7

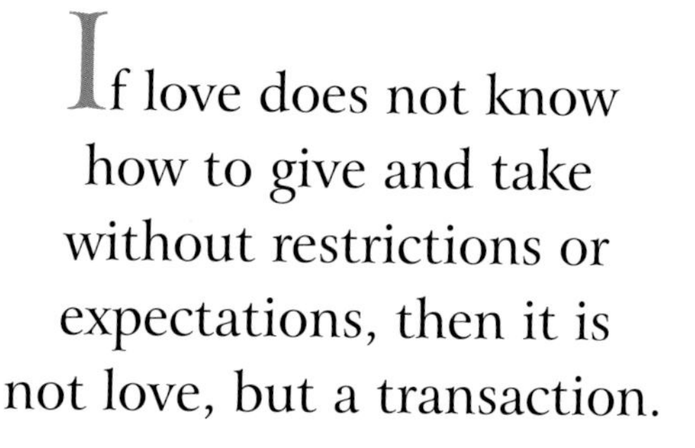

If love does not know
how to give and take
without restrictions or
expectations, then it is
not love, but a transaction.

EMMA GOLDMAN (1869-1940)

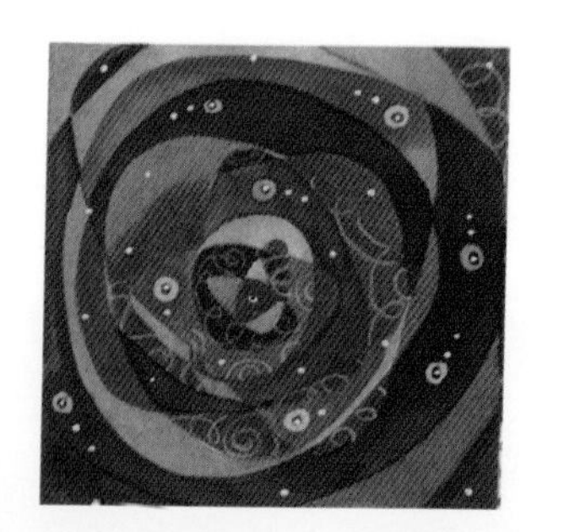

April 28

Treasure the love that you receive above all. It will survive long after your gold and good health have vanished.

OG MANDINO

September 6

The greatest waste
one can leave behind in life
is the love
that has not been given.

AUTHOR UNKNOWN

For a lot of us love is
the central drama of our lives.
It's the thing for which we take
inconceivable risks and make
moral decisions that we can't imagine
ourselves making.

ANITA SHREVE, FROM "A WRITER'S LIFE"

September 5

Two lovely berries moulded on one stem:
So, with two seeming bodies, but one heart.

WILLIAM SHAKESPEARE (1564-1616), FROM "A MIDSUMMER NIGHT'S DREAM"

A marriage makes of two
fractional lines a whole;
it gives to two purposeless
lives a work, and doubles
the strength of each
to perform it.

MARK TWAIN (1835-1910)

September 4

A woman who is loved always has success.

VICKI BAUM (1888-1960)

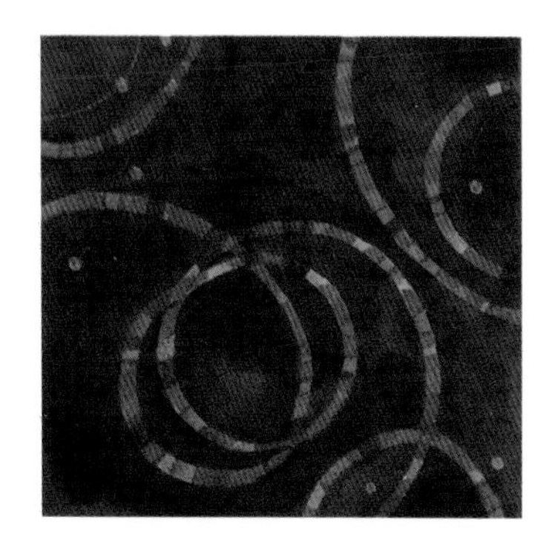

Oh, the miraculous energy that flows between two people who care enough to take the risks of responding with the whole heart.

ALEX NOBLE

September 3

Love is when
you can spend a day together
doing nothing in particular
– and be supremely happy.

PAM BROWN, B.1928

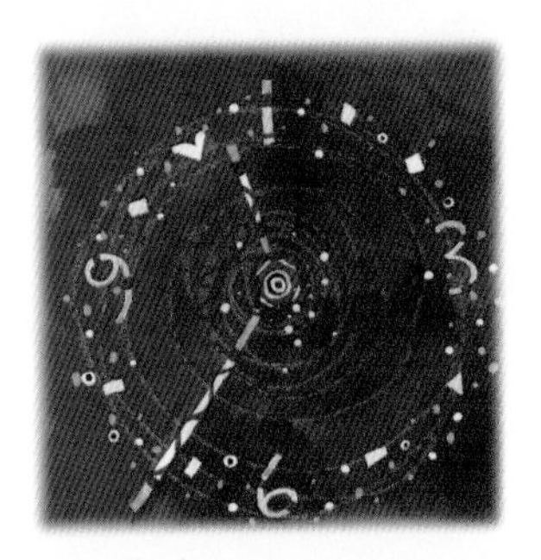

May 2

Two things cannot alter,
Since Time was, nor today:
The flowing of water;
And Love's strange, sweet way.

JAPANESE LYRIC

September 2

Everybody's the same
when it comes to love....
When someone in the ghetto
falls in love she hears bells –
the same bells someone
uptown hears
when she falls in love.

BERRY GORDY, B.1929

May 3

Him I love more than I love these eyes,
more than my life, more by all mores....

WILLIAM SHAKESPEARE (1564-1616), FROM "TWELFTH NIGHT"

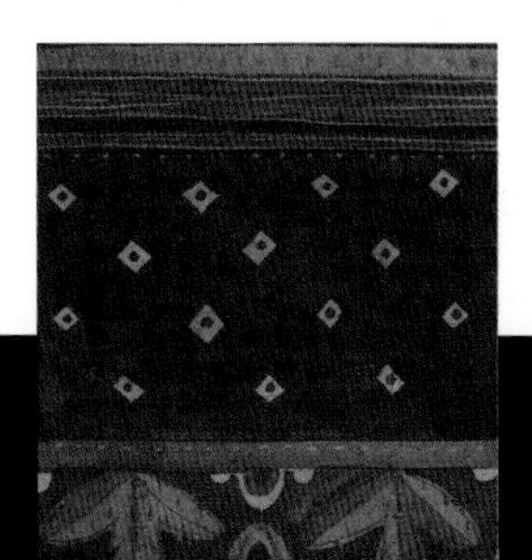

September 1

In you alone my desires give birth to delirium,
in you alone my love bathes in love.

PAUL ÉLUARD (1895-1952)

May 4

Knowing
is the most profound
kind of love,
giving someone
the gift of knowledge
about yourself.

MARSHA NORMAN

August 31

How silver-sweet sound
lovers' tongues by night,
Like softest music
to attending ears!

WILLIAM SHAKESPEARE (1564-1616),
FROM "ROMEO AND JULIET"

Breathless, we flung us on the windy hill,
Laughed in the sun, and kissed the lovely grass.

RUPERT BROOKE (1887-1915)

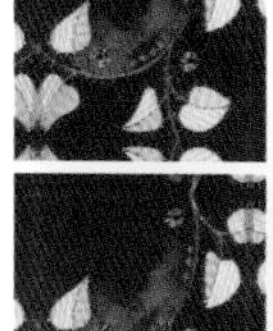

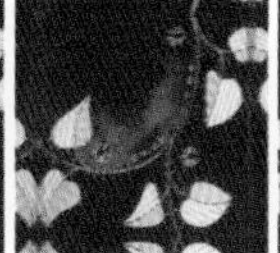

August 30

As long as one can admire and love, then one is young forever.

PABLO CASALS (1876-1973)

Love is the only light
that can truly read
the secret signature of the other person's
individuality and soul.

JOHN O'DONOHUE

August 29

All the goals and targets
in the world mean nothing unless you're happy,
you love and you're loved.

DARIUS DANESH

May 7

Days are more precious
waking up
with someone you love.

CARLY SIMON

August 28

I love you for the part of me that you bring out.

ROY CROFT (1907-1973)

May 8

The heart has its reasons
which reason knows nothing of.

BLAISE PASCAL (1623-1662)

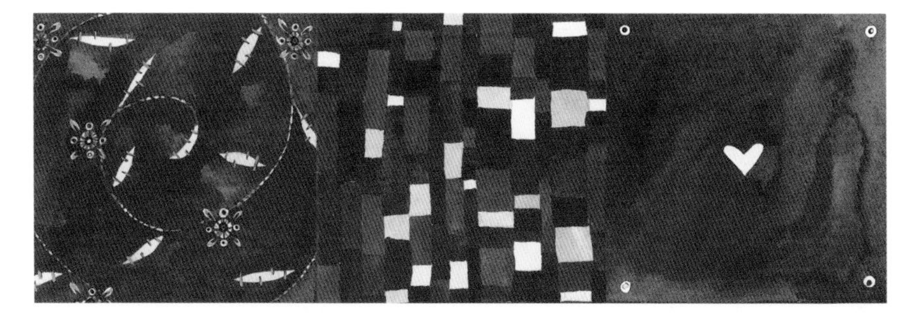

August 27

Love...
makes one little room,
an everywhere.

JOHN DONNE (1572-1631),
FROM "THE GOOD MORROW"

There is only one element in life
which is worth having at any cost,
and it is love. Love immense
and infinite, broad as the sky
and deep as the ocean –
this is the one great gain in life.
Blessed is he who gets it.

SWAMI VIVEKANANDA (1863-1902)

August 26

If I had a single flower
for every time I think about you,
I could walk forever
in my garden.

DIANE ACKERMAN

May 10

If we are lacking in love, real love – the kind that spends itself unreservedly on another – we accomplish nothing.

THE MONKS OF NEW SKETE

August 25

There is only one happiness in life, to love and be loved.

AMANDINE AURORE LUCIE DUPIN (GEORGE SAND) (1804-1876), IN A LETTER TO LINA CALAMATTA

May 11

But there's nothing
half so sweet in life
As love's young dream.

THOMAS MOORE (1779-1852)

August 24

Love is something eternal – the aspect may change, but not the essence.

VINCENT VAN GOGH (1853-1890)

May 12

I do not think we can ever
adequately define
or understand love;
I do not think we were ever
meant to.
We are meant to participate
in love without really
comprehending it.
We are meant to live
into love's mystery.

GERALD G. MAY

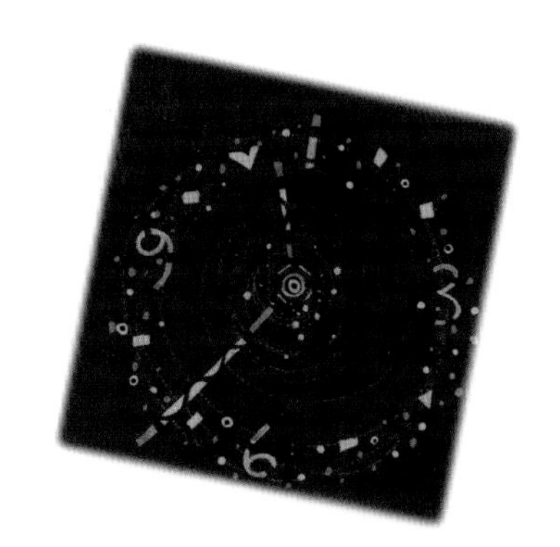

August 23

In dreams and in love there are no impossibilities.

JANUS ARONY

Truly loving another means letting go of all expectations.

KAREN CASEY

August 22

A happy couple share a certain smile that no one else quite understands.

PAM BROWN, B.1928

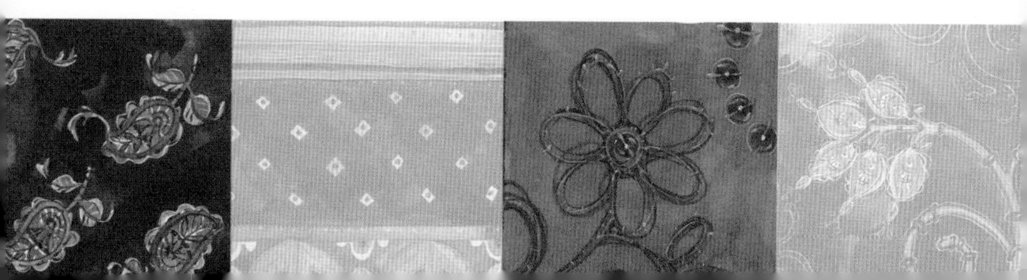

May 14

Happiness, when love adds one to one, is not doubled but multiplied a thousand times.

STUART & LINDA MACFARLANE

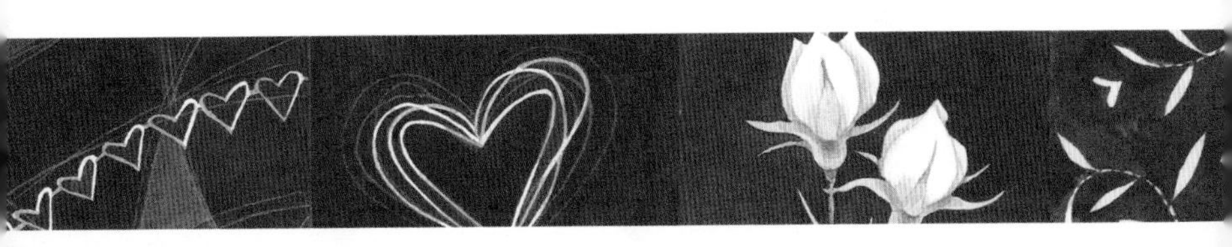

August 21

When a man loves a woman
and that woman loves him, the angels leave heaven
and come to their house and sing.

BRAHMA KUMARIS

May 15

You have intensified
all colours, heightened
all beauty, deepened
all delight.
I love you more than life,
my beauty, my wonder.

SIR ALFRED DUFF COOPER (1890-1954),
TO HIS FUTURE WIFE DIANA, 1918

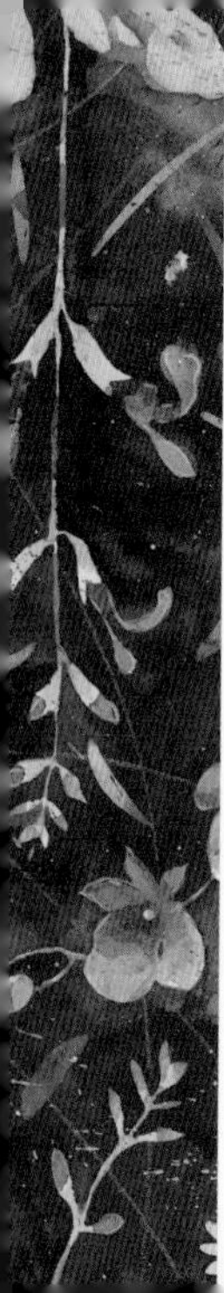

August 20

Darling, you want to know what I want of you. Many things of course but chiefly these, I want this thing we have inviolate and waiting – the person who is neither I nor you but us.

JOHN STEINBECK (1902-1968), TO HIS WIFE GWENDOLYN

Friendship and love should be the safe regions where your unknown selves can come out to play.

JOHN O'DONOHUE

August 19

Hold tenderly that which you cherish.

BOB ALBERTI

May 17

To experience love
in ourselves and others,
is the meaning of life.

MARIANNE WILLIAMSON, B.1952

August 18

Where thou art, there is the world itself.

WILLIAM SHAKESPEARE (1564-1616), FROM "HENRY IV"

May 18

When love floods the senses, it jams your sonar, blinds you to all else. Lightning might crash around you, eels and piranhas nibble at your toes and you don't care, because only One Thing matters – that longing which has overtaken your soul. We humans were made for that sweet, sweeping sickness.

SY MONTGOMERY

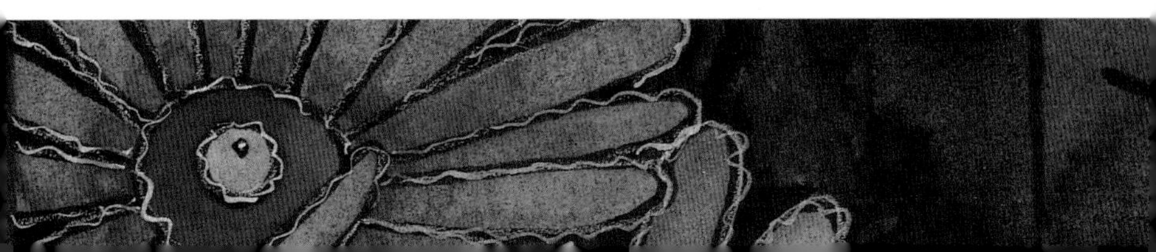

August 17

We must love one another, yes, yes, that's all true enough, but nothing says we have to like each other.

PETER DE VRIES (1910-1993),
FROM "THE GLORY OF THE HUMMINGBIRD"

May 19

Each year that's gone has brought us new kinds of happiness – may every year to come bring even greater joy.

PAM BROWN, B.1928

August 16

You are everything I need.
You are the sun,
the air I breathe.
Without you, life wouldn't
be the same.
Please never go away.
And if you go,
then don't forget
to take me with you.

BASIA

May 20

Love is a plant of tenderest growth:
treat it well, take thought for it and it may grow
strong and perfume your whole life.

FRANK HARRIS (1856-1931), TO RITA (ERIKA LORENZ)

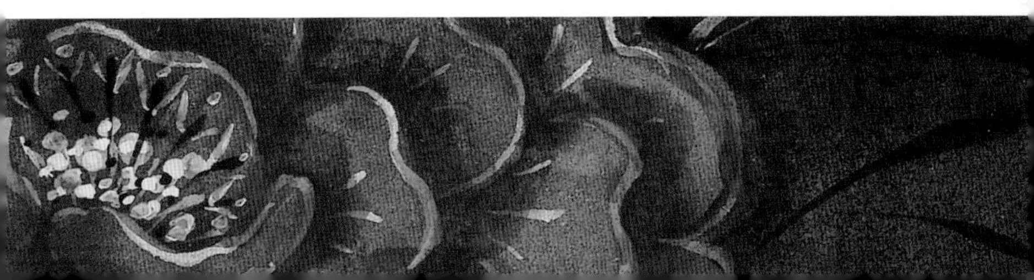

August 15

The course of true love never did run smooth.

WILLIAM SHAKESPEARE (1564-1616),
FROM "A MIDSUMMER NIGHT'S DREAM"

May 21

Love begets life.
Life begets love.

STUART & LINDA MACFARLANE

August 14

I know your eccentricities, your moods. And somehow, for some reason I can never fully understand, I am crazy with love for you.

CHARLOTTE GRAY, B.1937

May 22

Love is everything it's
cracked up to be.
That's why people are so cynical
about it....
It really is worth fighting for,
being brave for, risking everything for.
And the trouble is, if you don't risk
anything, you risk even more.

ERICA JONG, B.1942

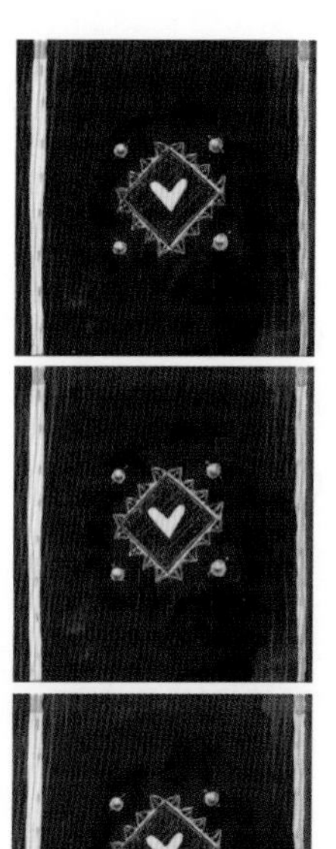

True love speaks in tender tones
And hears with gentle ear,
True love gives with open heart
And true love makes no harsh demands
It neither rules nor binds.

AUTHOR UNKNOWN

May 23

Accustom yourself to continually make many acts of love, for they enkindle and melt the soul.

SAINT TERESA OF ÁVILA

August 12

To love someone means to be involved with,
to identify with, to engage with,
to suffer with and for them, and to share their joys.

WILLARD GAYLIN

May 24

An orange on the table,
your dress on the rug, and you
in my bed, sweet present
of the present, cool of night,
warmth of my life.

JACQUES PRÉVERT (1900-1977), FROM "ALICANTE"

August 11

We cease loving ourselves if no one loves us.

MADAME DE STAEL (1766-1817)

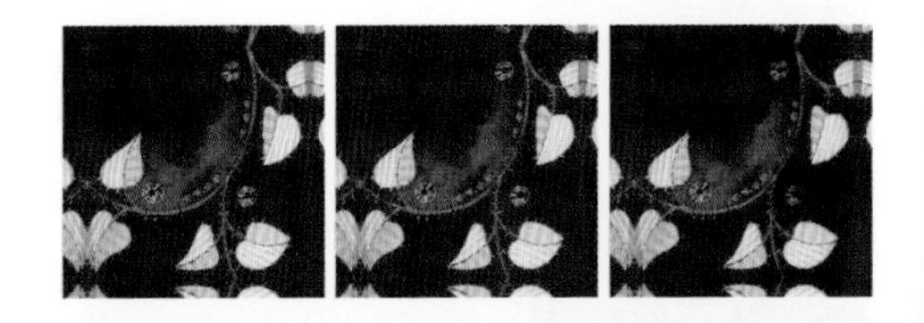

May 25

How glorious it is to live within your love.

PAM BROWN, B.1928

August 10

Nearly every one of us
is starving to be appreciated,
to be the recipient
of that most supreme
compliment – that
we are loved.

LEO BUSCAGLIA (1924-1998)

May 26

...it is in loving, as well as in being loved,
that we become most truly ourselves.
No matter what we do, say, accomplish,
or become, it is our capacity to love that
ultimately defines us. In the end,
nothing we do or say in this lifetime
will matter as much as the way we have
loved one another.

DAPHNE ROSE KINGMA, FROM "TRUE LOVE"

August 9

Love – bittersweet, irrepressible –
loosens my limbs and I tremble.

SAPPHO (655-610 B.C.)

May 27

Love...widens and enriches our life.

FRANZ KAFKA (1883-1924)

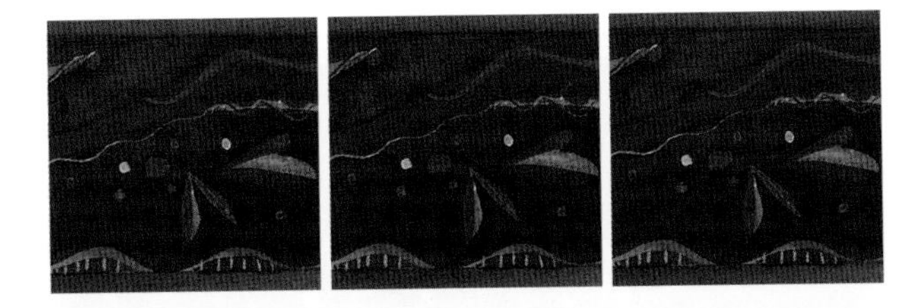

August 8

I love you as one must love:
excessively, to the point of madness and despair.
There are two things which
must never be mediocre: poetry and love....

JULIE DE L'ESPINASSE (1732-1776)

May 28

The one thing we can never get enough of is love. And the one thing we never give enough of is love.

HENRY MILLER (1891-1980)

August 7

We are crazy.
People have said it.
We know it.
Yet we go on.
But being crazy together
is just fine.

RAY BRADBURY, B.1920

May 29

In sandy earth or deep
in valley soil I grow,
a wildflower thriving
on your love.

FROM "SONG OF SONGS"

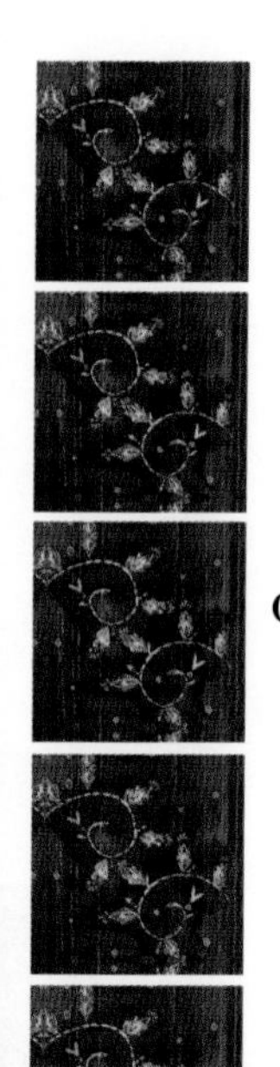

August 6

We do not know what excitements
or adventures, what dangers or amazements
lie ahead, or where the roadway leads.
But simply to travel in each other's
company is happiness
and certainty enough.

PAM BROWN, B.1928

May 30

How quickly bodies come to love each other, promise themselves to each other, without asking permission from the mind!

LORRIE MOORE, B.1957

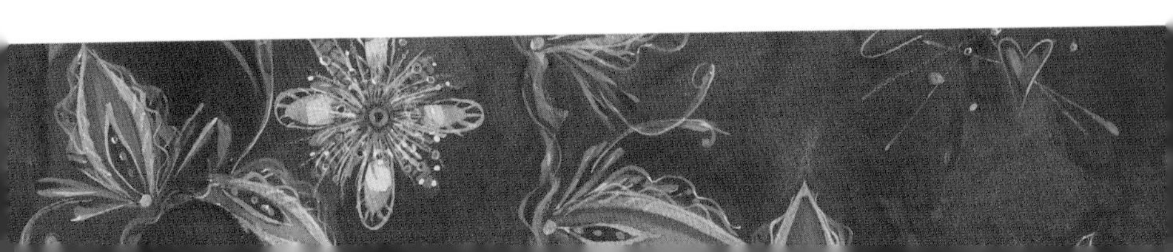

...love means that I am confident enough
about that other that I can trust him with my gift.

AUTHOR UNKNOWN

May 31

One of the most important things is to have love in your life; to give love and hopefully to be able to accept it.

EVA FRASER

August 4

We are bound by love to share all things, to explore the world together, to learn from each other, to discover compromise, and patience and a growing, deepening love.

MARION C. GARRETTY (1917-2005)

June 1

Love is what it is:
the most complicated, intense
and indefinable emotion.
And yet without it…
well, life wouldn't really
be worth living, would it?

MIKE GAYLE

August 3

All that we love
deeply becomes a part of us.

HELEN KELLER (1880-1968)

June 2

The act in bed is the mainstay of creation,
and it may satisfy the senses
but it does not feed the heart.
Love needs the instrument of a voice.

CATHERINE COOKSON (1906-1998)

August 2

I enjoy nothing without you.
You are the prism through which the sunshine,
the green landscape, and life itself, appear to me....
I need your kisses upon my lips,
your love in my soul.

JULIETTE DROUET (1806-1883), TO VICTOR HUGO

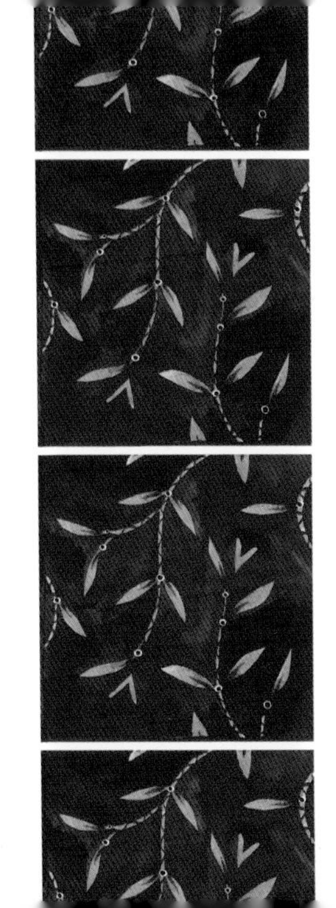

June 3

How comfortable
we are together,
Safe from the world
in mutual trust,
in love and friendship.

PAM BROWN, B.1928

August 1

The greatest beauty secret
of all is love.
To love and to be loved.
A woman in love
has a certain glow.

JOAN COLLINS, B.1933

June 4

Is there anything on earth more unearthly
than to be in love at eighteen?
It is like an abundant spring garden.
My heart was the Orient, and the sun rose from it;
I could have picked the stars from the sky.

JEAN STAFFORD (1915-1979)

Thou art to me a delicious torment.

RALPH WALDO EMERSON (1803-1882)

June 5

Young love.
It is the greatest thing.

DOROTHY PARKER (1893-1967)

What else is the world interested in?
What else do we all want, each one of us,
except to love and be loved, in our families,
in our work, in all our relationships?

DOROTHY DAY (1897-1980)

June 6

You trust the man you love
with every single part of you
...heart, body, soul, mind, life, bank balance,
worries, fears, secrets, hopes and dreams.

SIÂN E. MORGAN, B.1973

July 29

Your heart is an inexhaustible spring, you let me drink deep, it floods me, penetrates me, I drown.

GUSTAVE FLAUBERT (1821-1880),
TO LOUISE COLET

June 7

As we are, here,
together, now
and here,
Always you and I.

ROBERT GRAVES (1895-1985)

If I have the colic,
I take some medicine.
If I am seized by the pox,
I go down to the Hot-Springs.
But where is there help,
for what SHE does to me?

ETHIOPIAN LOVE POEM

June 8

...everything you do souses me, terrifies me, tortures me, elates me, everything you do is perfect.

PAUL ÉLUARD (1895-1952),
TO HIS WIFE ELENA DMITRIEVNA DIAKONOVA

THERE IS NO REMEDY
FOR LOVE BUT TO LOVE MORE.

HENRY DAVID THOREAU (1817-1862)

June 9

The heart that loves is always young.

GREEK PROVERB

July 26

It is more fun watching someone you love have fun than trying to have fun yourself.

RACHEL JOHNSON

Nothing is more mysterious,
mystical or magical than falling in love.

SARAH BAN BREATHNACH

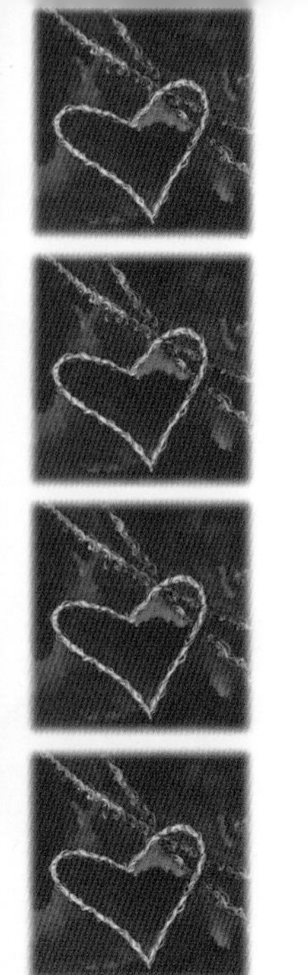

July 25

True love has no sides, limits,
or corners. It is without circumference
and beyond inside and out.
The heart of limitless love includes
all and everything, embracing one
and all in its warmth.
Genuine love is enough
in simply being itself.

LAMA SURYA DAS

June 11

Love is the strength that binds people together.
It is the most powerful thing of all.

BILLY MILLS

July 24

When two people are at one in their
inmost hearts,
They shatter even the strength of iron or bronze.
And when two people understand each other
in their inmost hearts,
Their words are sweet and strong,
like the fragrance of orchids.

CONFUCIUS (551-479 B.C.)

Love is enriched
by every good thing shared –
and made stronger by every sorrow
faced together.

PAM BROWN, B.1928

Nothing can be greater than love. Love is life, and life itself is spontaneous nectar and delight.

SRI CHINMOY (1931-2007), FROM "THE WINGS OF JOY"

June 13

I am at one with you. When we are together, I am content and relaxed in a way that I have never felt with any other person. Being with you is like being wrapped up in a warm, comfortable blanket of love.

STUART & LINDA MACFARLANE

July 22

I need your love
as a touchstone of my existence.
It is the sun which breathes
life into me.

JULIETTE DROUET (1806-1883),
TO VICTOR HUGO

June 14

I tell you, the more I think,
the more I feel that there is nothing more truly
artistic than to love people.

VINCENT VAN GOGH (1853-1890)

It is good to love as many things as one can, for therein lies true strength, and those who love much, do much and accomplish much, and whatever is done with love is done well. Love is the best and the noblest thing in the human heart, especially when it is tested by life.

VINCENT VAN GOGH (1853-1890)

June 15

The only thing
I know about love
is that love
is all there is....

EMILY DICKINSON
(1830-1886)

July 20

There's only one thing in this world that's worth having. Love. L-o-v-e. You love somebody, somebody loves you. That's all there is to it.

CHARLES MERGENDAHL

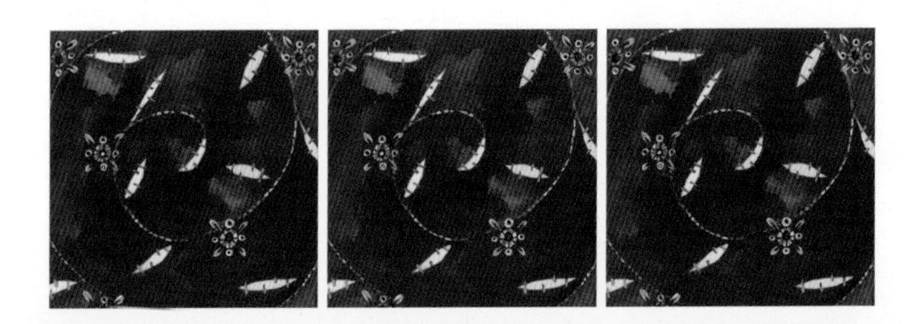

June 16

There were moments when I feared to hear your voice, and then I was disconsolate that it was not your voice. So many contradictions, so many contrary movements are true, and can be explained in three words: I LOVE YOU.

JULIE DE L'ESPINASSE, TO COMTE HIPPOLYTE DE GUIBERT, 1774

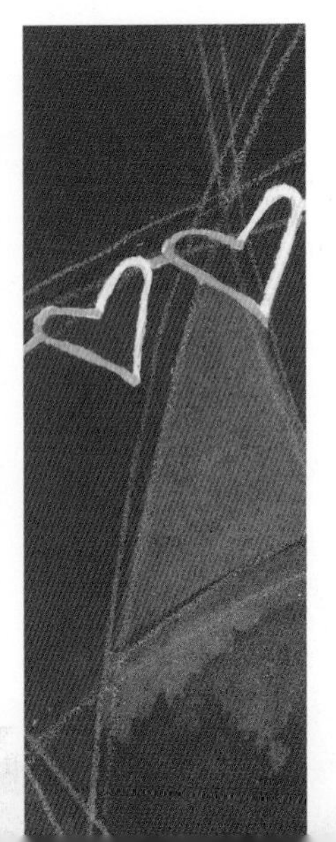

July 19

Come live with me
and be my love.

CHRISTOPHER MARLOWE
(1564-1593), FROM "THE BAIT"

June 17

Love is in ordinary things –
small kindnesses, a hand on the shoulder,
a kiss in passing.
A dish of strawberries.

CHARLOTTE GRAY, B.1937

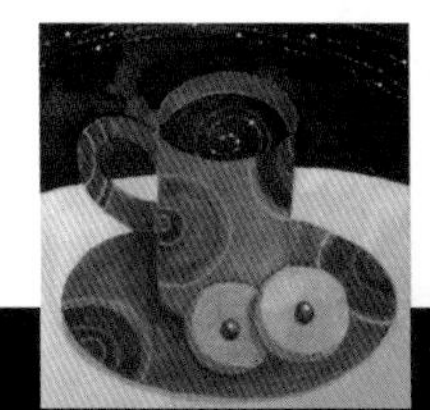

But love is a durable fire
In the mind ever burning;
Never sick, never old, never dead
From itself never turning.

SIR WALTER RALEIGH (1552-1618)

June 18

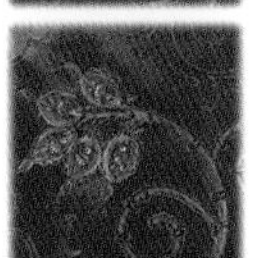

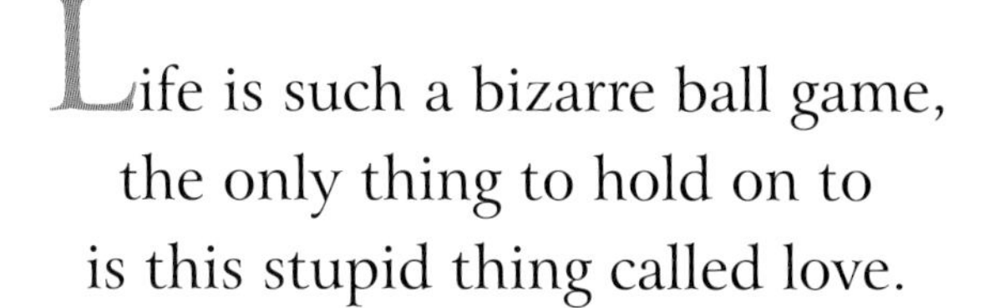

Life is such a bizarre ball game,
the only thing to hold on to
is this stupid thing called love.

ANDREW DUNCAN

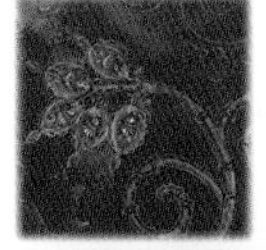

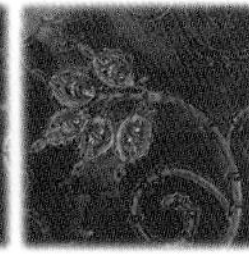

July 17

May we find strength that comes from unity, the quiet joy that comes from long companionship.

PAM BROWN, B.1928

June 19

Love is an irresistible desire
to be irresistibly desired.

ROBERT FROST (1874-1963)

July 16

Lovers re-create the world.

CARTER HEYWARD

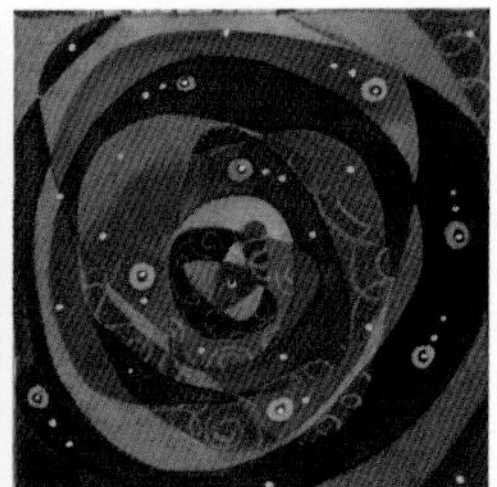

June 20

When one has once fully entered the realm of love, the world – no matter how imperfect – becomes rich and beautiful, for it consists solely of opportunities for love.

SØREN KIERKEGAARD (1813-1855)

July 15

...I have never known any union so sweet,
and beautiful, so spiritual and soul-satisfying as ours.
I swell in sunshine and my heart sings
with happiness.

LELLA SECOR (1887-1966)

June 21

First of all things,
there must be that delightful,
indefinable state called feeling at ease
with your companion, the one man,
the one woman out of a multitude
who interests you, who meets
your thoughts and tastes.

JULIA DUHRING

All pleasures should be taken
in great leisure and are worth
going into in detail;
love is not like eating a quick lunch
with one's hat on.

MAE WEST (1893-1980)

June 22

Lay in my arms till break of day
then tarry a little while longer.

LINDA MACFARLANE, B.1953

Oh, the comfort –
the inexpressible comfort,
of feeling safe with a person –
having neither to weigh thoughts
nor measure words,
but pouring them out.

DINAH MULOCK CRAIK (1826-1887)

June 23

You are always new.
The last of your kisses was ever the sweetest;
the last smile the brightest.

JOHN KEATS (1795-1821), TO FANNY BRAWNE

July 12

What is love?
Not to wish to exchange
a hut for a palace.

CHINESE PROVERB

June 24

Love isn't decent. Love is glorious and shameless.

ELIZABETH VON ARNIM (1866-1941)

July 11

Love cannot be defined
in one single term,
It cannot be taught and cannot
be measured.
It should always be handled carefully,
An eternal and precious gift
to always be treasured.

REDDY FOX

June 25

There is nothing you can do,
achieve or buy that will outshine the peace,
joy and happiness of being in communion
with the partner you love.

DRS EVELYN AND PAUL MOSCHETTA

July 10

Your voice
is the pillow on which
I rest my heart,
the blanket with which
I warm my dreams.

CHARLES GHIGNA

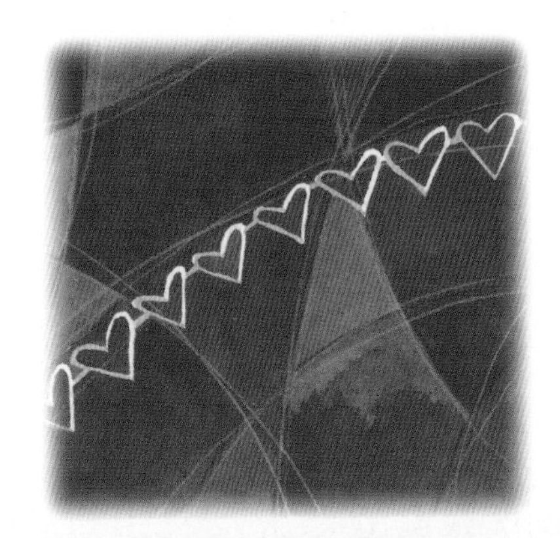

June 26

How can I count the kindness,
the astonishments, the joys that you have given me?
Your strength, your laughter,
the comfort of your arms.

PAM BROWN, B.1928

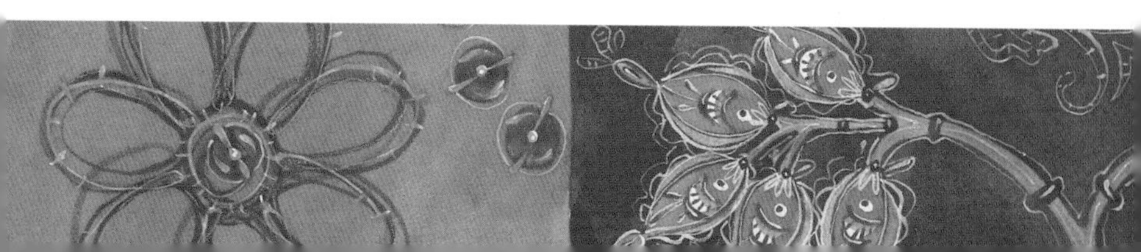

In the arithmetic of love, one plus one equals everything, and two minus one equals nothing.

MIGNON MCLAUGHLIN (1913-1983)

June 27

Time flies, suns rise, and shadows fall –
Let them go by, for love is over all.

FOUND ON A SUNDIAL

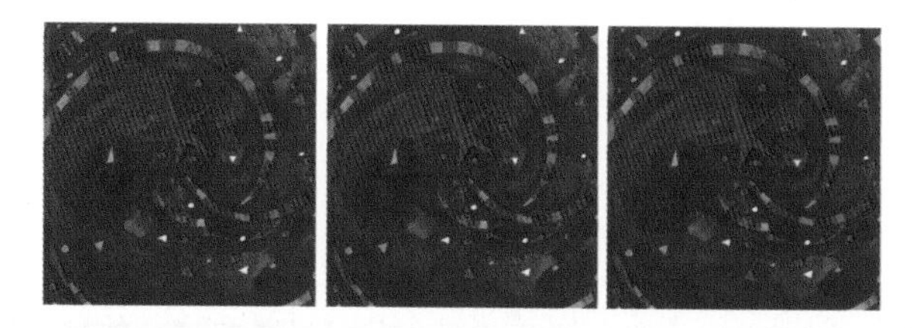

July 8

We think we love someone
for their looks; their walk,
maybe tone of voice, touch –
but when you analyse it, it is really
for their qualities – their warmth,
their humour, their intelligence,
kindness, etc....

JOYCE GRENFELL (1910-1979)

June 28

Love heals,
love is what makes
things a little better
than before.
Love is Universal.

BEARHEART (MUSKOGEE)
(1918-2008)

July 7

I did not know what love was till I met you. You taught me passion, showed me romance. And now I know life would be worthless without you.

LINDA MACFARLANE, B.1953

June 29

Shall I compare thee to a summer's day?
Thou art more lovely and more temperate.

WILLIAM SHAKESPEARE (1564-1616), FROM "SONNET 16"

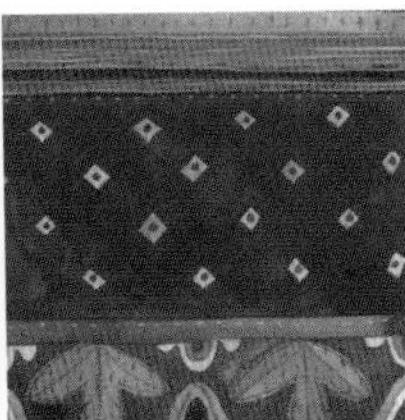

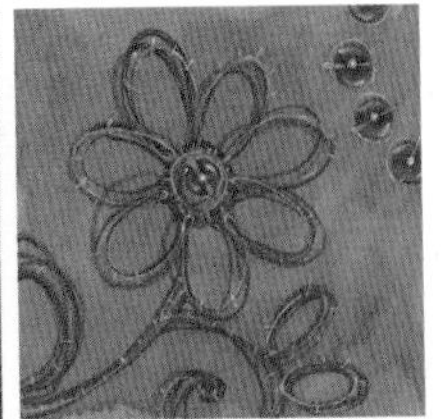

Certainly
I am happy
when the music
lifts the corner
of your mouth
and you smile.
Your hand is very
warm in mine
And you love me.

PADDI CLAY

June 30

We do amazing things for love:
take risks, conquer our fears
and our limiting beliefs –
all because of love.
It can truly create magic in our lives....

RICHARD PARKES CORDOCK,
FROM "MILLIONAIRE UPGRADE"

July 5

Love attracts love.

ANAÏS NIN (1903-1977)

If I were pressed to say
why I love him,
I feel that my only reply could be:
"Because it was he,
because it was I".

MICHEL EYQUEM DE MONTAIGNE (1533-1592)

Love's not Time's fool, though rosy lips and cheeks
Within his bending sickle's compass come;
Love alters not, with his brief hours and weeks,
But bears it out even to the edge of doom.

WILLIAM SHAKESPEARE (1564-1616), FROM "SONNET 116"

To live is to love.
To love is to live.

STUART & LINDA MACFARLANE

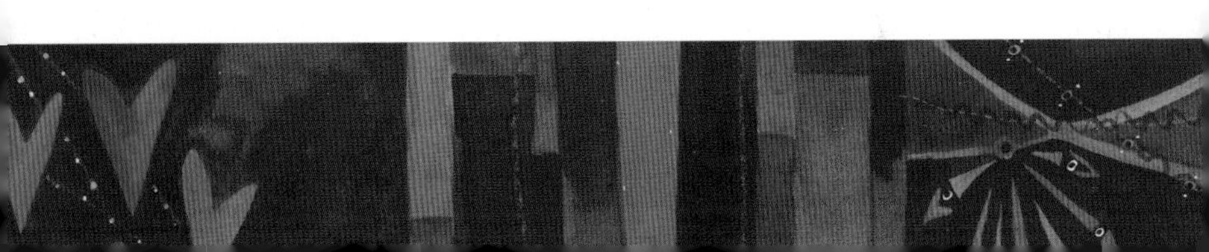

July 3

Without you, dearest dearest I couldn't see or hear or feel or think – or live – I love you so and I'm never in all our lives going to let us be apart another night. It's like growing old, without you. I want to kiss you so – I love you – and I can't tell you how much.

ZELDA FITZGERALD (1900-1948),
IN A LETTER TO HER HUSBAND F. SCOTT FITZGERALD

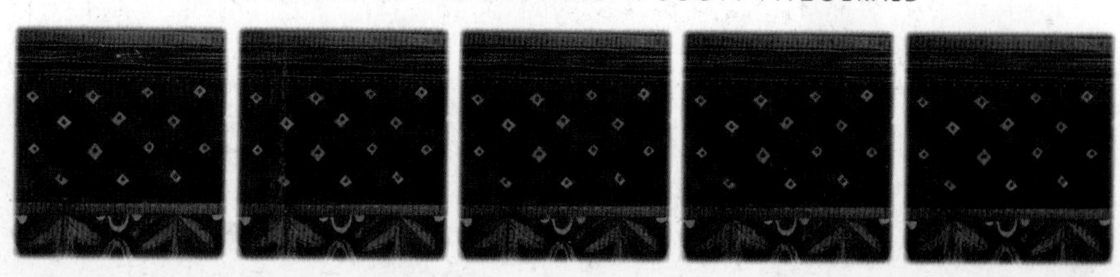